# Another World on Mask

*The Story of the World Cup Trout Fly Competition Angling on Ireland's Lough Mask*

By Denis Kelleher

# Another World on Mask

*A History of World Cup Trout Fy Competition Angling on Ireland's Lough Mask.*

*Written to commemorate the 50th anniversary of the An Tostal World Cup organised by Castlebar and District Anglers Association.*

First published in Ireland by Denis Kelleher, Neale Rd, Ballinrobe, in 2003. All rights reserved. No part of this publication may be reproduced, stored in a retrieval system or transmitted in any form or by any means, electronic, mechanical, photocopying, recording or otherwise, without the prior written permission of the publisher.

This book is sold subject to the condition that it shall not, by way of trade or otherwise, be lent, resold, hired out, or otherwise circulated without the publisher's prior consent in any form of binding or cover other than that in which it is published and without a similar condition including this condition being imposed on the subsequent publisher.

Copyright © D.Kelleher 2003

ISBN 0-9545283-0-1

# Table of Contents

| | Page |
|---|---|
| **Chapter 1 – The Fifties** | 19 |
| 1954 - Westport does it again! | 22 |
| 1955 - Easter on Lough Mask | 23 |
| When it was unlawful to fish on Sunday | |
| (Extract: *The Connaught Telegraph*, 25thApril 1954 Charles Russell) | 26 |
| 1956 - Grace Kelly's' World Cup at Whit Weekend | 27 |
| 1957 - A Winner from Ballyshannon | 29 |
| 1958 - Lough Mask. A Raging Storm, and a Mayo Footballer | 30 |
| 1959 - The Minister and the American Ambassador | 33 |
| **Chapter 2 – The Sixties** | 36 |
| 1960 - 1st and 3rd Prizes go Overseas | 36 |
| 1961 - Angler won Boat, Bride & World Title | 38 |
| 1962 - Return to Easter for the Tenth | 39 |
| 1963 - A Cold Start | 41 |
| 1964 - Robbie takes World Cup | 42 |
| The Jack Stack Era | 43 |
| Tom Coucill 1st Hon Secretary of the "World Cup" | 44 |
| 1965 - Transfer to Ballinrobe | 45 |
| 1966 - Munster Winner for 1st time | 48 |
| 1967 - Tony Mulloy as Secretary | 50 |
| Carraigín Dá Bhó | 51 |
| 1968 - To Westport once again | 52 |
| 1969 - Cup to Northern Ireland for 2nd time | 53 |
| **Chapter 3 – The Seventies** | 55 |
| 1970 - The Boatman is late | 55 |
| Changes Herald 1971 World Cup | 57 |
| 1972 - New Jetties at Cushlough | 58 |
| Local Committee member and International Angler wins 1973 World Cup. | 60 |
| 1974 - 12 inch limit is official | 61 |
| 1975 - World Cup for Dublin | 62 |
| 1976 – Robbie O'Grady for 2nd time | 63 |

| | |
|---|---|
| 1977 – "Jaws" Film Star participates in Festival | 65 |
| Controversy over Curraghmore Housing Scheme – Fears over effects of Arterial Drainage | 66 |
| 1978 - Return of the World Cup | 68 |
| 1979 - Another Day Added | 70 |
| **Chapter 4 – The Eighties** | 73 |
| 1980 - The Year of the Stockies | 73 |
| 1981 - A Winner from Derry | 75 |
| 1982 – Another Winner from Louth | 76 |
| 1983 – Sligo Angler wins World Cup | 78 |
| 1984 – World Cup for Germany | 80 |
| 1985 - Back to Westport Again | 82 |
| 1986 – World Cup for Fermanagh | 85 |
| 1987 – Kells, Co. Meath and World Cup Champions | 87 |
| The Rod Licence Dispute | 88 |
| **Chapter 5 – The Nineties** | 90 |
| 1991 – World Cup Returns | 90 |
| 1992 - A year of major growth | 91 |
| 1993 – Fishery Board Staff Member wins World Cup | 95 |
| 1994 – A Visit from Uachtarán na hÉireann | 96 |
| 1995 - The Wet Fly Dry Fly Controversy | 99 |
| 1996 – Another McLoughlin | 101 |
| 1997 - Year of Change | 103 |
| 1998 – A Successful Boat Manager | 106 |
| Tourism Angling Measure Plan | 106 |
| 1999 – Generous Sponsors | 109 |
| **Chapter 6 – To the Present and the Future** | 113 |
| 2000 – The Millenium Competition, A Second for *Derry* | 113 |
| The Competition of the Long Drifts | 115 |
| 2001 –Foot and Mouth Casts a Shadow | 117 |
| 2002 – A Good Year for Partry Schoolteacher | 120 |
| World Cup Catches Since 1953 | 123 |
| The Future | 126 |
| Early Records Lough Mask | 129 |

# Acknowledgements

Edited by
Seán O'Loughlin, Dr J.P. Hanrahan, Declan Kelleher

Graphics
Michael Walsh, Tuam

Mr Austin Vaughan and Ivor Hamrock, Mayo Co Library, Castlebar

The Connaught Telegraph.
The Western People
The Western Journal
The Mayo News
The Irish Times
Professor Phil Brookes, Luton, UK
Ruaidhri De Barra, Billy Murphy, Danny Goldrick,
Western Regional Fisheries Board.
Dr Martin O'Grady, Central Fisheries Board
Brian Geraghty, Bord Fáilte
Mr J.F. Stack, Westport
Garry Wynne "The Wynne Collection" Castlebar
John J. McGowan and Joe Hamrock, Castlebar
Dr Paddy McGowan, Limerick.
Dick Willis, Mallow
Esther Sweeney, Hon Sec. World Cup Committee, Ballinrobe
Orla Casey, Teagasc, Athenry

Photography
The author is extremely grateful to Tommy Eibrand for his photographs, the cover and throughout the book
Photographs: The Wynne Collection. Liam Lyons, Westport, Frank Dolan, Tricia Forde

I wish also to acknowledge the assistance and support I received from my wife Bernie and daughters, Elizabeth, Vanessa and Denise who also supplied technical assistance. Also, Ray Owens, my angling partner who made a number of useful suggestions.

# LOUGH MASK: WORLD CUP

My first reaction to the competition concerned – the name.

"These fellas don't suffer an inferiority complex anyway,' thought I to myself "The World Cup, mind you! They don't sell themselves short in Mayo!!"

*Brian Geraghty*

Like some of our politicians over the years, I then had time for mature reflection. "Why shouldn't they", I quickly concluded, "for where else can there be wet fly fishing for natural wild brownies to equal the Irish limestone loughs. Fair play to Ballinrobe and their friends from Castlebar – they knew what they had and were not afraid to label it properly.

The World Cup Competition and long weekend is special. The quality of the organisation equals that of the fishing. A marvellous feat for a small community and congratulations are deserved all round. Please accept mine. I sincerely hope that at some time during the celebrations a mention is made of the late Attie McCormack who gave of himself so generously to make lough Mask's World Cup a date in the angling calendar not to be missed.

I first brought my good friend Bob Church to Ballinrobe many years ago, and later to the World Cup. I don't believe he has missed it since. He tells me it's the fishing and the overall social ambience of the weekend that draws him back like a magnet. I don't swallow that at all . . . no sir, I know the attraction is that never-to-be-forgotten rendition of the "Rhinestone Cowboy" . . . You won't believe it, but I even think he genuinely likes listening to Robbie, and no doubt The Corrageen Cuckoo will swing into gear one more time.

May the great event go from strength to strength, and all you good people of Ballinrobe, stand and take your bow!!

**Brian Geraghty**
Bord Fáilte

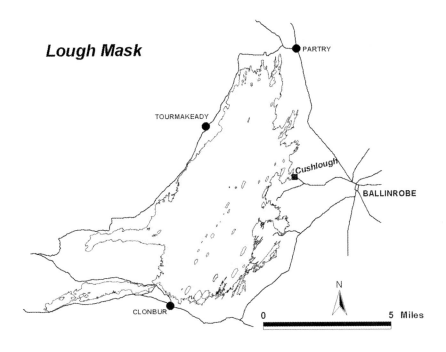

*1955 – Paddy Howard, Chairman, presents World Cup to Dr. Paddy McGowan, Castlebar.*

# Lough Mask

Lough Mask covers an area of 8275ha (20431 ac). The eastern shore of the lake is carboniferous limestone while on the west the geology is far more complex. The rock types range from Silurian quartzite to Ordovician slates. Outcrops of pre Cainozoic basalts which are poor in silica occur, as also do Ryolites and other volcanic rocks which are rich in silica. There are also Lower Avonian/Carboniferous shales and sandstones on the western side of Lough Mask. The limestone on the eastern shore has eroded much more so than the harder rocks on the west leading to the development of a much fretted shoreline with many promontories, bays and islands. The western shoreline is much more uniform in character. The surface of the lake is 62 feet above sea level and at its deepest point it reaches a depth of 208 feet.

Up until sometime in the late 18th century or early 19th century Lough Mask fish population consisted of brown trout, arctic char, sticklebacks, minnows and eels. The introduction of pike and perch had a negative impact on the trout stocks in that pike are the only true freshwater predator fish found in Irish waters. Perch compete with trout for food and habitat. In recent years a roach population has established itself in the lake. Roach also compete with trout for food and habitat.

Lough Mask is classified as one of the premier wild brown trout fisheries in Europe. To maintain it as such the Western Regional Fisheries Board has adopted a fisheries management policy aimed at ensuring that Lough Mask will continue to be so classified. To achieve this objective the Board carries out a stock management programme aimed at controlling both predator and competitor species in the lake. Data are available to show a correlation between the numbers of pike removed from a trout fishery and the concomitant increase in rod caught trout.

In order to ensure the maximum production of wild brown trout the Board has carried out major stream habitat enhancement works over the last nine years. The bulk of this work was funded under the Tourism Angling Measure (TAM). Improving and enhancing stream habitat will protected the genetic integrity of the wild brown trout population in that each stream makes a unique contribution to the parent fishery. The introduction of hatchery reared trout, albeit the progeny of Lough Mask fish, into streams other than their natal streams would compromise the genetic integrity of the Lough Mask wild brown trout population.

To further improve the trout angling on Lough Mask the Western Regional Fisheries Board has been instrumental in establishing the River Robe Catchment Management Committee. By implementing catchment management procedures and policies involving all of the stakeholders within the Robe catchment it is envisaged that the River Robe and its tributaries will be restored to productive levels that will over time make a valuable contribution to the trout stocks in Lough Mask and that the river itself will again be a viable trout fishery in its own right.

The World Cup Trout Angling Committee have over a period of forty nine years run a highly successful event on Lough Mask. The records of the numbers of anglers and the numbers of fish caught during each of the annual competitions has provided valuable data on the quality of the trout angling on Lough Mask. The Western Regional Fisheries Board acknowledges the value of these data and would like to congratulate the committee on their work and to wish them every success in future years in the running of this prestigious angling event.

*Ruaidhri de Barra*

*A group of competitors from County Meath celebrate Brian Moran's win, 1991.*

# The Winners of Lough Mask's World Cup Competition 1953 - 2003

| Year | Winner |
|------|--------|
| 1953 | Jack Stack, Westport, Co Mayo |
| 1954 | John McManus, Westport, Co Mayo. |
| 1955 | P. McGowan, Castlebar, Co Mayo. |
| 1956 | Leo Joyce, Westport, Co Mayo. |
| 1957 | John Gormley, Ballyshannon, Co Donegal |
| 1958 | Jim MeGowan, Castlebar, Co Mayo. |
| 1959 | D. Halton, Cootehill, Co Cavan. |
| 1960 | R. Phelan, London. |
| 1961 | A. Foley, Dromahair, Co Leitrim. |
| 1962 | J. Cox, Westport, Co Mayo. |
| 1963 | Michael Tolan, Crossmolina, Co Mayo. |
| 1964 | Robbie O'Grady, Ballinrobe, Co Mayo. |
| 1965 | Frank Smyth, Drogheda, Co Louth. |
| 1966 | Dick Willis, Mallow, Co Cork. |
| 1967 | R. Maharg, Belfast, Co. Antrim, N.I. |
| 1968 | Pat O'Connell, Westport, Co Mayo |
| 1969 | Jim Telford, Co Antrim. N.I. |
| 1970 | Winston McConville, Armagh, N.I. |
| 1971 | Dermot Treacy, Sligo. |
| 1972 | George Allister, Lisburn, Co Antrim. N.I. |
| 1973 | John J. Duffy, Kilmaine, Co Mayo. |
| 1974 | Tom Rice, Dublin. |
| 1975 | Pat Doheny, Rathgar Ave, Dublin. |
| 1976 | Robbie O'Grady, Ballinrobe, Co Mayo. |
| 1977 | Des Elliott, Dublin. |
| 1978 | C. W. Gibson, Crooked Wood, Mullingar |
| 1979 | John Jennings, Ballinrobe, Co Mayo. |
| 1980 | Louis Brennan, Tuam, Co Galway. |
| 1981 | Karl J. Henry, Draperstown, Co. Derry N.I. |
| 1982 | Jim Stafford, Dundalk, Co. Louth |
| 1983 | Brendan Smith, Sligo. |
| 1984 | Kurt Menrad, Germany. |
| 1985 | Joe Berry, Westport, Co Mayo. |

*Cushlough Bay.*

| | |
|---|---|
| 1986 | Brian Hallett, Belleek, Co. Fermanagh, N.I. |
| 1987 | Hughie McLoughlin, Kells, Co Meath. |
| 1988, '89, '90 | Cancelled, Rod Licence Dispute. |
| 1991 | Brendan Moran, Kells, Co Meath. |
| 1992 | Sean McGuire, Garrison, Co Fermanagh. N.I. |
| 1993 | Frank Reilly, Headford, Co Galway. |
| 1994 | Derry Ryan, Carlow. |
| 1995 | Gerry Cairns, Caherdavin, Limerick |
| 1996 | Noel McLoughlin, Kells, Co Meath. |
| 1997 | Padraig Munroe, Partry, Co Mayo. |
| 1998 | Craig Murray, Ballyclare, Co Antrim, NI. |
| 1999 | Billy Graham, Banbridge, Co Down. N.I. |
| 2000 | Derry Ryan, Carlow. |
| 2001 | Richard McDermott, Cloontrim, Co Longford. |
| 2002 | Tom Byrne, Partry, Co Mayo. |

# Prologue

*"Were it not that full of sorrow*
*From my people forth I go-*
*By the blessed sun, 'tis royally*
*I'd sing thy praise, Mayo"*

(An Tostal, 1953)

Little did this exiled poet of long ago imagine that, centuries later, anglers would be converging on Mayo from all quarters to participate in the World's Trout Fly Fishing Competition. With its much-indented coastline, Mayo typifies the scenic grandeur and variety of Ireland's western seaboard. Here is Nature in its grandest aspect, mountain and moorland, lovely landscapes and superb seascapes, but it is in her great lakes that Mayo is supreme as far as the rest of Ireland is concerned. Lough Mask, the largest lake in the County is also the venue for the annual World Cup Trout Fly competition. It is an extremely picturesque expanse of water over 10 miles long and 4.5 miles wide, is bordered by the Partry mountains almost entirely on the western shore and some of the peaks of the Maamturk range can be seen also from the lake in a southerly direction.

My earliest recollection of preparations for An Tostal festivities in 1953 was the painting of our neighbours' wall in a green colour, which I did not regard as overly attractive at the time. An Tostal gave it's name to one of the forty shades of green and "Tostal" green paint could be purchased in a large number of small hardware shops in our towns and villages for a long time afterwards. An Tostal was celebrated by hosting cultural and sporting events throughout the country and special An Tostal committees were established. The Ireland of the 1950s would not be regarded as a particularly colourful one and emigration was rampant. Perhaps the thinking behind the celebration of An Tostal was to eliminate some of the gloom and doom that an economically depressed economy visited on the country at that time. In Co Mayo every club and organisation of note had arranged attractive programmes to ensure the success of what was seen as our first National Festival. In Castlebar the late Paddy Howard and Gussie Wynne decided to visit Tom Coucill with a different idea in mind to mark the celebration of An Tostal in that part of the country. All three had a common interest in trout angling and were prominent officers of a very active Castlebar Trout Anglers Association.

# SOUVENIR

OF THE

## FIRST WORLD TROUT FLY FISHING COMPETITION

UNDER THE AUSPICES OF THE

### CASTLEBAR AND DISTRICT TROUT ANGLERS' ASSOCIATION.

VENUE : LOUGH MASK, CO. MAYO, EIRE.

## EASTER, 1953

THE FIRST PRIZE WINNER, FOR THE HEAVIEST WEIGHT OF FISH, RECEIVES VOUCHER FOR £250, WITH OSCAR AWARD AND PERPETUAL TROPHY AND REPLICA (Presented by the Castlebar and District Trout Anglers' Association).

THE SECOND PRIZE WINNER, FOR THE SECOND HEAVIEST WEIGHT OF FISH, RECEIVES VOUCHER FOR £150, WITH PERPETUAL TROPHY AND REPLICA (Kindly presented by the Management of the Castlebar Bacon Co. Ltd.).

THE THIRD PRIZE WINNER, FOR THIRD HEAVIEST WEIGHT OF FISH, RECEIVES VOUCHER FOR £75, WITH PERPETUAL TROPHY AND REPLICA (Kindly presented by the Management of the New Ireland Assurance Co.).

HEAT WINNERS WILL ALSO BE PRESENTED WITH PRIZES AT THE FINAL RECEPTION.

THE SPECIAL PRIZE WINNER, FOR THE HEAVIEST SINGLE FISH FOR THE WHOLE COMPETITION, RECEIVES A TROUT ROD (Kindly presented by the Management of Millard Bros., Ltd., Dublin).

No competitor can win more than one prize.

Connaught Telegraph Printing Works, Castlebar

# HEAT 1.
## SATURDAY, APRIL 4th, 1953
### LIST OF COMPETITORS.

| | |
|---|---|
| John Armstrong ......... **Castlebar** | Walter Leary .................. **Dublin** |
| John Bailey .................. **Galway** | Brian MacCapaid ......... **Dublin** |
| P. Barrett ............... **Lahardane** | Dr. Hugh A. McCaffrey **Lurgan** |
| Cpt. R. M. L. Baxter **Kent, Eng.** | James McCaffrey .......... **Lurgan** |
| W. A. Brookes ...... **Derby, Eng.** | Brian McCormack ...... **Castlebar** |
| Eugene Byrne ................ **Offaly** | James McCormack ...... **Castlebar** |
| John Canning .................. **Barna** | Tomas Mac Flanncada **Conamara** |
| Thomas Clancy ............... **Carna** | Michael McGovern ...... **Garrison** |
| I. J. Clarke ............... **Rossmuck** | Michael McLoughlin ... **Westport** /4 |
| Col. Hastings Clay **Skipton, Eng.** | Miss Emily E. P. MacManus |
| Thos. Clydesdale ................ **Cork** | **Pontoon** |
| J. Comerford ............... **Longford** | J. MacManus ............... **Westport** /5 |
| Leo M. Conway ............. **Dublin** | Jack MacManus ........... **Dublin** |
| Alex. Corcoran ......... **Lahardane** | P. J. McNamara ........ **Longford** |
| // Sydney Costello ......... **Westport** | Rev G. Martin ............. **Galway** |
| P. J. Coughlan ............. **Athlone** | Mr. J. Meldon ......... **Kent, Eng.** |
| Dr. B. T. Cullen ............. **Cavan** | Robert G. Moffett ........... **Cork** |
| B. Daly .................. **Ballinrobe** | Tom Molloy ......... **Tourmakeady** |
| J. Dempsey ......... **Ballyshannon** | Batholomew J. Monaghan |
| Charles Donohoe ......... **Galway** | **Oughterard** |
| Martin Egan ............... **Athlone** | Geo. T. Moore ............. **Dublin** |
| F. Feeny ..................... **Longford** | P. T. Moran ............. **Castlebar** |
| Dr. A. J. Fitzgerald ... **Roscrea** | J. Baldwin Murphy ......... **Clones** |
| Martin Gibbons ............... **Clones** | Supt. M. Neville ...... **Oughterard** |
| R. Gillespie ............... **Castlebar** | Denis O'Boyle ...... **Letterkenny** |
| V. S. C. Gloster ...... **Limerick** | Colm O'Conaill ............. **Cork** |
| Oliver D. Gogarty, S.C. **Dublin** | T. J. O'Connor ............. **Dublin** |
| P. F. Goodwin ............. **Clones** | Thos. Val. O'Connor **Swinford** |
| H. J. Waldron Hamilton | Malachy O'Hare ...... **Ballinrobe** |
| **Roscommon** | W. R. O'Kelly ............. **Galway** |
| Mrs. K. Hannon ......... **Foxford** | James P. Rowley ......... **Swinford** |
| Sean Hannon ............... **Foxford** | Hugh Ruddy ............. **Ballina** |
| /2 N. W. Hewetson ......... **Westport** | J. Ryan ........................ **Cork** |
| John Sylvester Higgins **Longford** | James Henry Smith ...... **Ennis** |
| Templeton C. F. Holder ... **Boyle** | Lt.Col. A. O'B. Traill **Bushmills** |
| Thomas Horkan ............ **Foxford** | M. C. Vernon ............. **Roscrea** |
| Evan H. Jonathan **North Wales** | G. T. Walker ................ **Cork** |
| Jack Keenan .................. **Dublin** | Wm. J. Waters ................ **Cork** |
| Michael Kelly ............... **Newport** | William W. Williams ... **Dublin** |
| John Kevlighan ...... **Ballymote** | G. Wynne .................. **Castlebar** |
| /3 John J. Lohan ........... **Westport** | |

The Draw for this Heat will take place on Friday, April 3rd, 1953, at 9 p.m., in the Imperial Hotel, Castlebar.

The Competition will commence at 11.30 a.m. and end at 6 p.m. on Saturday, April 4th, 1953. The Starting Point will be Cushlough Bay, Ballinrobe.

The 10 Best Rods will compete with the Best Rods from Heat No. 2 on Easter Monday, April 6th, 1953.

Weight of Fish from this Heat does not go forward to the Final.

# HEAT 2.
## SUNDAY, APRIL 5th, 1953
### LIST OF COMPETITORS.

| | |
|---|---|
| Michael Armstrong ... **Castlebar** | Sean McCann ............... **Ballina** |
| M. Berry ............... **Westport** | Gerald McCormack ... **Castlebar** |
| Josie Bourke, Senr. ... **Castlebar** | Joseph McCormack ... **Castlebar** |
| Matt Bourke ......... **Tourmakeady** | Dr. John McDarby ... **Ballinrobe** |
| Dr. P. Bresnihan ...... **Castlebar** | Rev. Fr. McEnnis ...... **Castlebar** |
| Patrick Browne ............ **Foxford** | Myles McGing ............ **Westport** |
| Peter Browne ............ **Foxford** | Edward McGowan ...... **Chicago** |
| Thomas Byrne, B.D.S. **Swinford** | Jack McNeely ............... **Ballina** |
| P. G. Claffey ............ **Castlerea** | Andrew McNeely ......... **Ballina** |
| Thos. Coucill ............ **Castlebar** | J. Mellett ............... **Castlebar** |
| Dr. R. G. Cronan ......... **Newport** | Bernie Molloy ............ **Ballina** |
| Patrick Davitt ............ **Swinford** | M. Mongavan ......... **Castlebar** |
| Martin Dever ............ **Castlebar** | Dr. E. Mongey ......... **Castlebar** |
| Peter Dever ............ **Castlebar** | Arthur Moran ............ **Ballina** |
| John Dillon-Leetch **Ballyhaunis** | Dr. B. Moran ............ **Castlebar** |
| C. J. Doherty, M.P.S.I. **Westport** | Dr. Matt Moran ......... **Castlebar** |
| Matthew Donnelly ......... **Dublin** | Michael Moran ............ **Castlebar** |
| Liam D. Dunn ......... **Newbridge** | Michael Moran, T.D. **Castlebar** |
| Fred Dunne ......... **Ballyhaunis** | Patrick B. Moran ...... **Castlebar** |
| Maurice Dunne ......... **Castlebar** | Bernard Mulcahy ... **Dungarvan** |
| Thos. P. Flanagan ... **Castlebar** | Dr. Harry O'Carroll **Manorhamilton** |
| J. Finan ............... **Kiltimagh** | |
| Michael Gavin ............ **Castlebar** | P. O'Connell ............ **Westport** |
| Bernie Gillespie ......... **Castlebar** | John O'Donnell ......... **Westport** |
| Thomas Gillespie ...... **Castlebar** | Conn O'Driscoll ......... **Castlebar** |
| John Gibbons ............ **Westport** | Dr. Edward O'Hara ...... **Foxford** |
| C. Hanley ............... **Castlebar** | M. J. O'Hara ............ **Foxford** |
| M. Heverin ............... **Castlebar** | Thos. G. Perry ............ **Belmont** |
| W. W. Hewetson ...... **Westport** | Cpt. Jourbert F. Powell **Roscrea** |
| Patrick Higgins ......... **Westport** | Patrick Quinn ......... **Castlebar** |
| T. F. Hynes ............... **Castlebar** | George Smith ............ **Castlebar** |
| William L. Hynes ... **Ballyhaunis** | Terence D. Spillane ...... **Dublin** |
| Henry De Jong ............ **Holland** | J. Stack ..P.u.C............ **Westport** |
| M. J. Kelly ............... **Castlebar** | Roger Thomas ............ **Castlebar** |
| R. W. Kelly ......... **Claremorris** | A. V. G. Thornton ...... **Castlebar** |
| Ed. Kennedy ............ **Swinford** | J. Tuohy ............... **Ballintubber** |
| T. A. Lavelle ............ **Castlebar** | Rep. United Drug Co. ... **Ballina** |
| Martin Lyons ............ **Castlebar** | Patrick J. Vahy ... **Claremorris** |
| M. J. Lyons ............ **Westport** | G. E. Wilson ... **Manorhamilton** |
| Jack Murphy ............... **Ballinrobe** | |

The Draw for this Heat will take place on Saturday, April 4th, 1953., at 9 p.m., in the Imperial Hotel, Castlebar.

The Competition will commence at 11.30 a.m. and end at 6 p.m. on Sunday, April 5th, 1953. The Starting Point will be Cushlough Bay, Ballinrobe.

The 10 Best Rods will compete with the Best Rods from Heat No. 1 on Easter Monday, April 6th, 1953.

Weight of Fish from this Heat does not go forward to the Final.

# 2nd WORLD TROUT FLY FISHING COMPETITION

## LOUGH MASK, COUNTY MAYO

### EASTER WEEK-END—APRIL 17, 18, 19, 1954

Sponsored by Castlebar and District Trout Anglers' Association, under the auspices of the I.T.F.F.C.C.

## PRIZES

1st PRIZE—**FORD POPULAR CAR**, with Challenge Cup, Replica and An Tostal Oscar Award.

2nd PRIZE—**16ft. BOAT** and **SEAGULL OUTBOARD ENGINE (with Clutch)**, and Challenge Cup presented by Castlebar Bacon Co. Ltd.

3rd PRIZE—**SEAGULL OUTBOARD ENGINE (with Clutch)**, and Challenge Cup presented by New Ireland Assurance Company.

Also Trout Rods, Reels and other Valuable Prizes.

**ALL ABOVE PRIZES ARE NEW.**

Connaught Telegraph, Castlebar.

# CASTLEBAR AND DISTRICT TROUT ANGLERS' ASSOCIATION.

## OFFICERS :

**President**—Mr. P. T. Moran.

**Vice-Presidents**—Messrs. J. P. McCormack and T. P. Flanagan.

**Chairman**—Mr. P. Howard.

**Hon. Sec.**—Mr. T. Coucill.

**Hon. Treasurer**—Mr. C. Hanley.

**Committee**—Messrss B. Gillespie, R. Gillespie, G. Smith, G. McNally, C. O'Driscoll, G. Wynne, M. Dunne, P. Quinn, I. Kelly.

**Weigh-in Stewards**—Sergt. Glynn and Mr. D. Carroll.
**Official Timekeepers and Referees**—Rev. Dean Jackson, Messrs. P. J. Quinn and T. P. Flanagan.

## MAYO COUNTY ANGLING CLUBS' REPRESENTATIVES :

**Loughs Conn and Cullen**—Messrs. B. Gallagher and C. Warde.

**Crossmolina Anglers**—Major White, J. Tolan.

**Ballina Anglers**—G. Mulloy, J. Rice.

**Swinford Anglers**—T. Byrne, E. Kennedy.

**Westport Anglers**—P. O'Connell, J. Stack.

**Tourmakeady Anglers**—T. Mulloy, Dr. Browne.

**Foxford**—S. Hannon, M. Howley.

**Newport**—M. Kelly.

**Ballinrobe**—J. J. Leydon, B. Daly.

# Seventh World Trout Fly Fishing Competition

| 1953 | 1954 | 1955 |
|---|---|---|
|  |  |  |
| J. STACK | J. MacMANUS | L. JOYCE |

## WORLD CHAMPIONS 1953—1958.

| 1956 | 1957 | 1958 |
|---|---|---|
|  |  |  |
| DR. P. McGOWAN | J. GORMLEY | J. McGOWAN |

(Photos—G. Wynne, Castlebar).

*organised by the*
**CASTLEBAR AND DISTRICT TROUT ANGLERS' ASSOCIATION**

**COMMENCING WHIT SATURDAY, 16th MAY, 1959.**

**Venue: LOUGH MASK**
CUSHLOUGH BAY, BALLINROBE, CO. MAYO, EIRE.

# Chapter 1

The Castlebar Club was set up in 1928 and total membership for 1952 was 41. The fact that 21 committee meetings took place in that year would indicate that it was a very vibrant club. Release of fry from the hatchery in Pontoon to Loughs' Conn, Carra, Tuckers', and Church had taken place and the club was hosting the National championships on Lough Mask on 16th May 1953. The "Inland Fisheries Trust Inc" was set up in 1952 by Government for the development of angling, in particular brown trout angling in Ireland and one of the first operations undertaken in the west was the transfer of trout from Lough Feagh near Newport to Lough Conn in a joint operation with the Castlebar Club. Paddy Howard and Gussie Wynne met Tom Coucill and told him of their great idea, namely a competition on Lough Mask with 500 pounds in prizes. Tom enthusiastically agreed to the idea and immediately rallied to their aid the local and national Press and Radio. Paddy Howard, who was chairman of the Club, had earlier distinguished himself as a member of Irelands' International team, by winning the International for Ireland on Lough Leven and becoming Ireland's

*Chairman of Castlebar Trout Anglers Association Paddy Howard, with Micheál Ó Móráin, T.D. and Revd A. O'Toole on left.*

captain for that year. Arrangements were made with the Boatmens' Association on Lough Mask for the provision of boats for the event.

The Committee of Castlebar and District Anglers were as follows: President: Mr P. T. Moran; Vice-Presidents: J. P. McCormack and T. P. Flanagan; Chairman: Paddy Howard; Hon. Sec.: Tom Coucill; Hon. Treasurer: C. Hanley; Committee: B. Gillespie, R. Gillespie, G. Smith, G. McNally, C. O'Driscoll, G. Wynne, M. Dunne, P. Quinn, I. Kelly; Weigh-in Stewards: Sergt. Glynn and D Carroll; Official Timekeepers and Referees: Rev. Dean Jackson, P. J. Quinn and T. P. Flanagan.

In an editorial in *The Connaught Telegraph* on June 6th 1953 reference was made to the event as follows: "By far the biggest event, however is the International angling competition commencing on Saturday April 4th (Easter Saturday). A grand and very representative entry has been attracted for the event including anglers from abroad, and in thus attracting visitors, the Castlebar club has succeeded in fulfilling the object behind An Tostal far better than has any other club, association or organisation in Mayo, perhaps in Ireland. Far more is it to their credit indeed that the idea behind the attractive event was not merely one of popularising competitive angling; neither was it, unlike the majority of clubs, one of making money – in fact the club will lose by it, believe it or not."

*The Connaught Telegraph*, published a booklet for the occasion with the official An Tostal stamp bearing the inscription "An Tostal" April 5th-26th 1953 (Ireland at home) and advertising the "World Cup" on Lough Mask. Nine Co Mayo angling clubs were listed in the publication and in addition to Castlebar the three most closely identified with Lough Mask were listed with the following representatives. Westport Anglers: P. O'Connell, J. Stack; Tourmakeady Anglers: T. Molloy and Ballinrobe & District Anglers: J. J. Leydon, B. Daly.

John Hynes, County Jeweller, Castlebar supplied the "World Trout Fly Fishing Competition Perpetual Cup" for the event and 50 years later the same cup adorned with the names of all winners on the base is one of the most sought after prizes in Irish angling.

Paddy Howard and his committee made the necessary arrangements for the inaugural competition and the late Mr M. Moran T.D., later to become a Minister had sought extension to closing hours for the final international banquet in the Imperial Hotel. A very interesting exchange had taken place between himself and the Judge.

Mr Moran: "As I have stated it will be an unusual type of dinner because of the fact that the competitors will have to go to their own hotels and then come on to Castlebar. There are special circumstances in this case as, for instance, the competitors will have to change out of the great number of pullovers that are necessary for braving the storms of Lough Mask and then would only arrive in Castlebar at closing time".

Judge replies: " They will not be fishing in the dark. If I give this you will be back next year telling me that I gave it last year".

Mr Moran, also a keen angler was successful in his application, which was granted until 11.30pm, and the day was saved. Peter Browne, a second-generation from Inish Coog remembered his father taking the boat out of the shed in preparation for the competition with snow on the ground. The Qualifying heats were run over 2 days with 82 anglers competing each day and 58 fish were weighed in. A northeast wind drove snow over the lake at times and the hills on every side of the lake were inches deep in snow. Among those who braved it out for the full fishing time were three octogenarians, namely 87 year old P. T. Moran, Castlebar, 84 year old Mr McGovern from Garrison and 83 year old J. Meldon from Kent. One must remember that the era of super light carbon fibre rods had not even been dreamt about at this stage and split cane and greenheart rods were likely to be the order of the day. Following the final on Easter Monday in which 20 anglers participated in brighter weather conditions, the anglers were rowed back to Cushlough Bay by the hardy boatmen of Lough Mask. For the record 5 fish were weighed in for the final. 7 countries were represented in this competition and the winner was the late Jack Stack of Westport with one fish of 2 lbs 2ozs. A system

*Jack Stack, Westport. 1st Winner of World Cup Competition 1953.*

of substitutes prevailed and the second placed Mr M. Mongavaun whose sub was Mr S.J. McCormack, Castlebar with 2 fish for 1lb 12ozs.

Among those present at the International Banquet in the Imperial Hotel in Castlebar was Mr Gerald Bartley, Parliamentary Secretary to the Minister for Agriculture. At the final banquet a Mr George Waters from Cork made reference to the fact that the oldest man in the room was Mr P.T. Moran, President of the Castlebar Anglers. He also apologised for the fact that there were not more anglers from Munster. There were six entries from Munster and he had trained two of them and both got into the final, but unfortunately at Moran's hotel in Ballinrobe the hospitality was so great that they dined well but wined unwisely. Although they did fish next day the bags were empty. Forty five anglers from Castlebar competed and the four anglers from Ballinrobe were: The late Bernard Daly, Malachy O'Haire, Dr J. McDarby and Jack Murphy.

I have not succeeded in finding any reference to the enormous role which must have been played by the boatmen in an era which did not include outboard engines as all movement was by use of oars and this must have taken huge effort on a lake of Masks' stature. Of necessity, the distance an angler could hope to cover, especially in rough weather must have been greatly reduced. However, far from being confined as an event, which was organised for An Tostal in 1953, the competition was to become an annual event that became increasingly popular.

## 1954 – Westport does it again!

A colleague of mine who lived in Westport at this time recently expressed his amazement to me that a World competition could be won on two successive years by Westport anglers. Indeed the town has the distinction of providing no less than 5 winners of this event. What singled out the 2nd World Cup Competition which took place over the Easter weekend from all others was that a "Ford Popular" car sponsored by Josie Bourke and Son, Castlebar was added to the challenge cup, replica and An Tostal Oscar award for 1st prize-winner. Second prize was a 16' boat and Seagull Outboard Engine with clutch and challenge cup presented by Castlebar Bacon Company and third was a "Seagull" Outboard engine with clutch and (Wc 9/2 the weigh-in gets underway) challenge cup presented by New Ireland Assurance Company. This year also there would be a dinner after each heat as well as the final.

At a meeting of the club the secretary Tom Coucill read a letter from the secretary of Lough Mask Boatmen's Association stating that 50 or more boats would be available for the competition if required.

A former Westport Employment Exchange Manager the late John McManus emerged as overall winner from 164 entries, 100 of which were from outside the county, with a catch of 3 fish weighing 4 lbs 14.5ozs and was also the winner of the heaviest fish with an individual fish weighing 3 lbs 4.75ozs. Mr McManus also won his Heat with 3 fish weighing 3lbs 7.5ozs and certainly performed a "fifties" version of the Grand Slam in this competition. The other Heat winner was the late Maurice Walsh of Ballinrobe with 4 fish weighing 3 lbs 14.3ozs.

*The Connaught Telegraph* reported that when the news of Mr McManus' win trickled through Westport on Easter Monday evening the town was all agog with excitement and delight, especially in John's Row where Mr McManus resided. Mr Verdon Clarke's broadcasting van paraded the streets announcing Mr McManus's success. Immediately there was a stampede of people to Westport Railway Station followed by a fleet of motorcars, as the champion would have to pass this point on his way back from Lough Mask. A triumphal parade then took place through Westport's streets led by Westport Brass Band to the Octagon where a huge reception was organised.

*The Connaught Telegraph* reported that the competition was held in ideal weather conditions. Fishing generally under the conditions obtaining was considered reasonably good for Lough Mask, and if the all-round catch was not as large as desirable, the average weight of fish caught was considered pretty good. The energetic secretary the late Tom Coucill was again singled out for special praise as were the Lough Mask Boatmen headed by Mr Finlay.

76 anglers competed in the heat held on Easter Saturday. While the legal size limit was 8 inches, the competition imposed a limit of 10 inches from the very start. Only 10 qualified for the final. A total of 88 competitors took part in Easter Sunday's heat with 12 qualifying places available. 22 anglers assembled at Cushlough Bay for the final on Monday morning. The day was reported as dull with the water rough and choppy and a total of 14 fish weighing 14lbs 15.25ozs were caught.

Among the comments made by Mr M. Moran TD at the final dinner in the Imperial Hotel, which was now well established as competition headquarters was that, " Eisenhower and Churchill have exchanged information on the A Bomb, and I don't see why those Westport fishermen would not exchange information with us". Referring to the competition Mr Moran said "I did bring in a fish but I believe Mr Flanagan and Dean Jackson, the weigh-in stewards, discovered it was radioactive: - at least I got a very poor reception when I brought it up to the scales". A special feature of the competition in these early years was "The Sweep". Cards were issued at an early stage and apparently most people had a go at trying to guess who would be the outright winner. Overall statistics for the competition were: 164 anglers caught 93 trout weighing 97 lbs - 5ozs.

## 1955 – Easter on Lough Mask

Members of the Castlebar Club commenced arrangements to host the 1955 World Cup on Lough Mask at an early stage and competition dates were set at Easter weekend April 9th, 10th and 11th. Tom Coucill once more played a leading role as Secretary of the event and the Lough Mask Boatmen allocated of 45 boats for the event. The draw was set for the Imperial Hotel on Good Friday. In the same year a Westport man, Mr Norman Hewetson was appointed Captain of the Irish International Team and the Rev. Dean Jackson, Tuam was elected as President of the Irish Trout Fly Fishing Committee. Joining Mr Hewetson on the Irish Team were the late Paddy Howard and Martin Phelan of Castlebar. Lough Mask Boatmen's Association held a meeting to make final arrangements for boatmen for the competition and also discussed repairs to Caher and Cushlough piers and the possibility of erecting swimming pools there.

*Dr. Paddy McGowan, Castlebar, winner of 1955 World Cup, pictured with his winning boatman, P. J. Malone.*

The Third World Cup competition proved to be just as successful as the first two. *The Connaught Telegraph* reported that the weather on Saturday when the first heat was held was anything but favourable to good fishing. Heavy rain lashed by a southwesterly gale continued through the day. On Sunday the wind veered north westerly and more fish were caught but were reported to be lighter. One of the competitors, Dr Paddy McGowan was fishing at the mouth of Farragher's Bay. He had recently commenced work as an intern at Castlebar Hospital and was anxious to prove his worth to two other angling brothers. He considered himself lucky because he had drawn a very keen boatman namely the late Tom Cusack and Tom had counselled that sticking to the shallow water and in the bays was likely to yield the best results at this early time of the year .One perhaps over zealous cast later was followed by a bang and the cane rod splintered into two pieces. Paddy, in despair, sought to make himself comfortable in the bottom of the boat and perhaps snatch 40 winks. Shortly afterwards, thinking of the 5 pounds he had borrowed to enter the competition, he took another look at the rod and decided to attempt a repair job. He succeeded in lashing the two ends together and commenced to cast very gently once again. By now Tom Cusack had manoeuvred the boat to a strategic position in Golden Bay, and up came one of those Golden Beauties that the bay must have got its name from and took Paddy's' fly. Following a long struggle during which the running repair job was severely tested, Paddy guided a 3 lbs and half oz trout to the net and qualified for the final day's fishing.

On Monday anglers and boatmen were confronted by a gale in the morning with the result that most of the fishing early in the day was confined to Cushlough Bay. Many of the boats were late starting, such was the fury of the westerly gales lashing the shore. The hardy and willing boatmen of Lough Mask as usual gave of their best and won the praise of all who met them. Paddy McGowan and his competing partner T. J. Cleere were drawn with boatman P. J. Malone.

Following a quick conference in the boat P. J. decided to venture close to the mouth of Cushlough and endured some heavy weather before starting a drift in the general direction of Martins' Island. Towards 4 p.m. in the evening the official boat complete with an outboard engine approached and Paddy Howard enquired if there were any fish caught. Dr McGowan reported 4 fish of approx. 3 and a half lbs weight. Paddy had already visited most of the boats in the area and informed him that he was in pole position. Immediately a more excited Dr McGowan commenced casting as if he had not fished for a week and rose a nice trout, but such was his excitement that he "struck hard" with the inevitable consequence of a break in the cast. Some time later there was a repeat performance and he was wishing that Paddy Howard had motored in the direction of Tourmakeady rather than coming near him. There was a large crowd on the lakeshore when the boats put out but the attendance was small compared to the vast throng that gathered in the evening when the boats were coming in. Word had reached the shore by 5.45 pm that the boat in which Dr McGowan was fishing had the biggest catch. Soon the weigh in was underway and there was prolonged cheering when it was announced that Dr McGowan had the heaviest catch, weighing in 4 fish for 3 lbs - 5.5ozs. In 2nd place was Mr Michael Horkan, Swinford with 3 fish 1lb - 14ozs and third T. J. O'Connor, Dublin 1 fish 1lb - 7.5ozs. Looming ominously in 4th position was another Westport man whom I had the pleasure of knowing for many years, namely the late Leo Joyce. I have it from a very reliable source that the winning flies were a green and golden olive especially tied for the competition by Mr Jimmy McHale, New Antrim St. Castlebar.

Seventy-four competitors fished in the first heat on Saturday and the top 12 rods qualified for the final. The heat winner was R. Gillespie, Castlebar with 2 fish weighing 4 lbs - 8.5ozs. In the 2nd heat on Sunday 80 anglers competed and the heat winner was 1953 World Champion Jack Stack with 1 fish weighing 3 lbs 10.25ozs, 2nd was Luke Higgins, Ballinrobe with 3 fish weighing 3 lbs 4ozs. Last man to weigh in a fish on that day was none other than Robbie O'Grady, Ballinrobe who is a present member of the organising committee, but more about Robbie later.

*The Connaught Telegraph* listed 12 boatmen who accompanied the 24 anglers on the lake for the final as: John Burns, John Farragher, Peter Burke, Tom Cusack, Peter Cameron, P. Feeney, John Finlay, John Prendergast, P. J. Malone, M. Horan, Edward Finlay and Jim Burke. Overall statistics were: 154 anglers caught 91 trout weighing 96.47 lbs over the three days.

*1955 World Cup finalists.*

At the final dinner The President of the Castlebar Club Mr P. T. Moran stated that when the Central Tostal Council wrote asking for angling clubs to do something for the first An Tostal the Castlebar club volunteered to run a World competition which became more and more successful each year. The Committee had in mind the changing of the date from Easter to Whitsun, as at that time of the year there would be a prospect of getting more fish and more anglers. This announcement was made to the applause of the attendance. The Vice President Mr J. P. McCormack stated that it amused him to think of the changed attitude to fishing now and when he was a boy. At that time fishing was looked upon as the pastime of a corner boy or idler and often he ran the risk of parental wrath by stealing away to a river or lake for a few hours and on his return had to hide his rod and gear in the garden of his home. Since then the outlook changed to the extent that at present the sport of angling was classed as one for "gentlemen". I reproduce an article on Mr J. P. McCormack, which was written in his 75th year in the early 1950s which links the past with the previous century in angling terms and written by Charles Russell in *The Connaught Telegraph*.

**When it was unlawful to fish on Sunday**
(Extract: *The Connaught Telegraph*, 25thApril – Charles Russell)

The story begins on a May morning in 1889 when as a boy he often set off for Tucker's lake, adjacent to the town. He was armed with the innocent fishing paraphernalia popular in those days – a pole, some cord, a bent pin and a lunch bag in which the most important item was a box of blackheads. It was the Sabbath, all was at peace and the wee flaxen – haired gasúr cantered merrily along, the size of the catch looming larger before him as he neared his destination. Alas! cruel fate intervened and thereafter the whole course of his life was changed. Just below the Workhouse (as it was then), he was seized by two Peelers, his gear was taken and smashed, his lunch and precious blackheads trampled upon and he was encouraged on the return journey with a rise from a no. 11 in the small of the back. At the time it was a breach of the law to fish on Sunday, and of course our hero was a Fenian. There and then he solemnly vowed that as long as God gave him breath he would fish and shoot when he wished and where he wished.

He was privileged, as few have been privileged, to fulfil this vow. He fished in every preserved water in Mayo and shot in every landlord's estate in those bad old days when such breaches of etiquette were indictable offences. What is more, he got away with it. But in the strict sense of the word, he never took a fish illegally. He fished within season and with rod and line. He was too much the sportsman to do otherwise. In the 1950s he had become a legend in his own lifetime, his exploits ranking with the most daring in modern fiction. The personality in question was the late Mr John P. McCormack of Ellison Street, Castlebar. Then aged 75 years, but as a young man after his first disastrous fishing expedition he was as keen as ever. He was a founder member and President of the Castlebar Club, a President of the Carra Anglers' Club, a founder member and Chairman of the Castlebar Salmon Anglers' Club.

The following is an insight into what was available in terms of quality angling at the time. His best season on Beltra lake: 87 Salmon. Heaviest fish, 25.75 lbs, and his best rise of fish on the same water: 22 Salmon came to his flies in half an hour. He created a record there in 1959 when he landed 14 salmon in 4 evenings, lost three and struck a further seven. Best day's sea-trout fishing on the same water: 47 fish. Heaviest sea trout 4.75 lbs. Best day's brown trout fishing: 22 averaging over 2lbs each, rather strangely from Lough Cullen 1909. The bag he remembered most: 9 trout weighing 24lbs (three of 4lbs) (three of 3lbs) one of 2lbs and a pounder (Lough Mask 1926) Heaviest brown trout killed 6.5 lbs, Lough Conn 1911, Greatest number of trout killed in a day – 38 trout on Mask 1913. All these fish were taken on the fly. Trolling and Dapping for trout are of more recent origin! He fished that years World Cup and qualified for the final. He was Head of the firm of John P. McCormack & Sons Ltd, Building Contractors, Castlebar.

## 1956 – Grace Kelly's' World Cup at Whit Weekend

At the AGM of the club early in the New Year the proposal was adopted to change the competition from Easter to Whit weekend. Mr John Loftus from Crossmolina, a member of the club suggested that the World Cup competition be transferred to Lough Conn but the proposal was not seconded. A vote of thanks was passed to the Ballinrobe boatmen for their major contribution to the success of the event despite inclement weather.

*1956 World Cup finalists.*

Amidst reports of large trout caught from the Ballinrobe area of Lough Mask, John Finlay had an 11.5 lb trout, the late Jack Kelly, one of 12.5 lbs and a 4.5 lb caught by the late Martin Browne, the 1956 World Cup Competition was announced for Whit weekend 19th to 21st of May. Regular cross channel visitors entered at an early stage and an entry is recorded from as far away as Newfoundland. *The Connaught Telegraph* reports that Mayo's County town and its neighbouring town of Ballinrobe will be en fete during the weekend as they extend hearty greetings to the many visiting anglers who will journey from distant parts to take part in this event. There is also mention of a possible entry of 200. Headquarters for the event will be "The Travellers' Friend Hotel" where the draw will take place on Friday night and the dinners will be held after each competition.

The 4th annual World Cup competition proved to be the most successful in the series of world events. Even though not blessed by ideal fishing weather for the heats the catch was satisfactory. A record number of 178 anglers competed, and in Saturday's heat 86 anglers competed, 47 caught 109 fish weighing 87 1bs averaging .79 lbs, the winner was Leo Joyce of Westport with 2 fish weighing 4lbs 14.5ozs, 2nd was Willie Garvey with 4 fish weighing 4 lbs 6.25ozs and 3rd was Joubert F. Powell with 9 fish weighing 4 1bs 3.5ozs. 92 anglers fished the 2nd Heat and once more 1953 Westport World champion Jack Stack, won with a catch of 9 fish weighing 8lbs 13ozs. Second this time was Anthony O'Brien with 1 fish weighing 5lbs 5.25ozs. In third place Joubert F. Powell caught 9 fish weighing 4lbs 3.5ozs. The stage was set for the first World Cup final of Whit and what a final that was!

Following an eventful final during which the wind increased and angling conditions improved the fly invented by Jack Stack, namely the "Grace Kelly" proved to be a killer for the late Leo Joyce who became World Champion with a catch of 12 fish weighing 11lbs - 15ozs. Consistency among the top anglers was the order of the day. Leo had already won the Heat, and in 2nd position was Dr Paddy McGowan the 1955 World Champion with a catch of 3 fish weighing 7 lbs - 15.5ozs and in 3rd place was none other than Jack Stack, World Champion 1953 and already a heat winner in this competition with a catch of 9 fish weighing 7 lbs - 8.5ozs. This must surely rate as one of the most consistent performances of all time by these 3 anglers and the Fly named after Princess Grace of Monaco whose ancestry is from nearby Newport played a major role in the destiny of the 1956 World Cup.

## 1957 – A Winner from Ballyshannon

At the 1957 AGM of Castlebar Anglers the Hon. Sec. Tom Coucill congratulated Mr Pat Quinn Junior who, while fishing on Lough Mask with wet flies caught a 12-pound trout and won the All Ireland Tostal Plaque. The fish was declared champion of its class for 1957 and the *Field & Stream* magazine also presented the winner with a split cane rod. The World Cup competition was discussed. In addition to all the other prizes on offer the club decided that a special prize of £100 would be added to the prize schedule for the best overseas rod in an effort to attract an increasing number of overseas anglers and boost the local tourism economy. This would increase the prize fund to £600 for 1957. A considerable number of enquiries were received that year and a party of 8 had booked at an early stage. Enquiries and entries were received from Jamaica, Port of Spain, Colorado, France, Belgium, England, Scotland and Wales.

*A view of boats with competitors on their way to fish for World Cup.*

The 5th annual World Cup competition took place on 8th, 9th and 10th of June 1957 and for the first time the results reflected an international flavour. However, a double drowning tragedy took place on Lough Mask on the week before the competition in which a local man, Liam Biggins and Michael Cunningham from Ballyhaunis lost their lives whilst fishing on the lake. This was to cast a shadow over the competition. On Saturday morning 84 competitors lined up in their boats ready to start the competition joined with Rev. W. Elliott in reciting a decade of the Rosary and then observed a minutes silence as a mark of respect to the two men who were to participate in the competition.

The weather was reported as cold, though reasonably favourable, but the fishing was judged to be disappointing and not up to the standard of other years. Eighty four anglers competed in the first heat and E. Everard, Castlebar was heat winner with 5 fish weighing 5lbs 5ozs followed by John Gormley, Ballyshannon, 4 fish weighing 4lbs 1/4oz. and Dr H O'Carroll, Manorhamilton 2 fish 3lbs 11.25ozs. The 2nd heat accommodated 93 anglers and heat winner was G. Greer with 2 fish weighing 4lbs 10.25ozs followed by Robbie O'Grady with 3 fish 3lbs 10.25ozs and third C. J. Tyrch 1 fish 2lbs 11ozs. 21 qualifiers fished the final and John Gormley of Ballyshannon won the competition and became the 5th World Champion with a catch of 2 fish

weighing 2lbs 14.75ozs. In 2nd place was J. W. Matson, England with 3 fish. 2lbs 4.5ozs and 3rd was Mrs. Audrey Dewar also from England with one fish, 1lb 14ozs. Overall statistics were that 177 anglers competed and caught 134 trout weighing 129.6 lbs. The final banquet at the Travellers Friend in Castlebar had a truly international flavour about it and the club was proving to be successful in attracting overseas visitors with little help from the Irish Tourist Board.

## 1958 – Lough Mask. A Raging Storm, and a Mayo Footballer

At the AGM of Castlebar Anglers the chairman Mr Paddy Howard referred to the fact that the World Cup attracted more overseas visitors than ever before proving that it is going from success to success. He stated that it was a fact that they lost money but was quick to point out to all those who say that it is purely a local affair won each year by Westport or Castlebar that this is not so. "Last year (1957) three of the major prizes went abroad and the winner came from Ballyshannon." Secretary Tom Coucill announced that the 6th annual World Cup competition would take place on 24th, 25th and 26th of May 1958 and the dates would coincide with the peak of the mayfly hatch. He confidently forecast that last year's record entry of 177 would be broken once again. How right he was. A total of 205 anglers are reported to have entered, but I can only find evidence of 176 competing with 20 competitors from overseas. Perhaps the rough weekend took its toll on some of the competitors.

He also announced that anglers taking part should note that an Act came into force on that year making it illegal to take a fish less than 10 inches in length from the lake. To avoid mistakes every boat would be provided with a 10-inch rule. Headquarters for the event was the "Travellers Friend" Hotel. Among the guests at the final banquet would be Mr Erskine B. Childers, Minister for Fisheries and Mr Micheál O'Moran, Minister for the Gaeltacht who would also fish the competition.

The *Connaught Tribune* stated that the 6th World Trout Fly Fishing Competition held on Lough Mask that year lost none of its former greatness and was the big western sporting event held over the Whit weekend. Not alone had it the convivial atmosphere associated with this great event, but this year it can be said that never before was there such a spirit of sportsmanship and keenness displayed by the men and lady anglers who braved Lough Mask in a raging storm to take part in the competition. It was reported as the keenest and closest fought competition ever, as can be gathered from the fact that the difference of a quarter of an ounce weight of fish determined this year's World Cup Angling Champion.

A total of 87 competitors fished Saturday's Heat in a northerly gale with squalls of rain and hail, very cold and sometimes bright. The heat winner was John Burns, Ballinrobe with 4 fish weighing 6lbs 2ozs.and the winning boatman was J. Sullivan. In 2nd place was the 1956 World Champion Leo Joyce with 5 fish weighing 5lbs 2.5ozs and third was Charles Hanley, Castlebar with 6 fish 5lbs 1.5ozs. 38 competitors weighed in 67 fish for a total weight of 63lbs 13.5ozs. The first 10 anglers qualified for the final. On Sunday 89 rods took up the running in a gale force northwesterly wind. It was reported as cold and bright. P. Kelly, Westport won the heat with 2 fish weighing 4lbs 4ozs, 2nd Jack McCormack, Dublin and third, Kevin Loftus, Ballina. 33 competitors weighed in 76 fish for a total weight of 65lbs 18.5ozs.and the first 10 anglers qualified once again. When one considers that today, one angler in every 4 is guaranteed to qualify in the same competition, less than one in nine qualified in those days!

The final was fished in strong northwesterly wind, cold and bright. No doubt, the tin of canned luncheon meat provided by Castlebar Bacon Co. was much appreciated in these conditions. Possibly the youngest boatman on that day was 17 year old Joe Cusack of Cushlough who was doing his best to keep the boat on the proper drift because things were happening in this boat. Former Mayo senior footballer and member of Mayo Co. Council engineering staff Mr J. P. ("Tot") McGowan was having a good day. Mr McGowan recalled that night that during the day the boatman mistook him for his already famous brother Dr P. McGowan and when the going was tough as it was for most of that day, turned around and asked him " Doctor, would I strain my heart if I kept at this? The reply "No fear, Keep up the good work". Joe Cusack is now a prominent member of the organising committee of this event for many years and is a staff member of the Western Regional Fisheries Board. While he did not strain his heart, the vigorous rowing put considerable strain on the back of his trousers which eventually split.

Mr McGowan won the closely fought competition with 6 fish weighing 4lbs 15.5ozs – and attributed his success in no small measure to the boatman's co-operation. In 2nd place was that very consistent angler Jack Stack, Westport who made a wonderful bid to regain the cup and was just beaten at the winning post by a quarter of an ounce with 4 fish, 4lbs. 15.25ozs. Third was Sydney Costello with 6 fish weighing 4lbs 13.5ozs. Best lady was Miss Ann McMorrow, London.

*Sergeant H. Glynn presents the World Cup to Jim McGowan, Castlebar.*

Ninety-three year old president of the club Mr P. T. Moran, who despite the inclement weather had also competed, extended a special welcome to UK businessman Mr Jack Vincent, the blind overseas angler, who had competed for the first time from Maidenhead, and was reported to have fished with the greatest of ease and enjoyed himself. Mr Howard, Chairman of the club extended a word of thanks to the boatmen of Lough Mask and their chairman Mr John Burke who along with Tom Cameron were their guests at the dinner in the Travellers' Friend Hotel, Castlebar.

*Centre: Jim McGowan, Castlebar, World Cup Winner 1958 with 2nd placed Jack Stack and 3rd Sidney Costello, Westport.*

## 1959 – The Minister and the American Ambassador

The organisers of the World Cup have been encouraged by the number of competitors who return year after year. Typical was a party of anglers from Lancashire, which began as one rod in 1955 and had grown to five in 1959. Similarly Mr Jack Vincent, although he lost his sight in the last war, had acquired remarkable skill with a rod and line and enjoyed himself so well on the previous year that he had already entered a party of four for the current competition. At this stage the problem of the organisers was no longer seen as the future of the competition, rather how to make it more representative of overseas countries, and one of their disappointments to date had been the failure of Bord Fáilte to help with overseas publicity. A major change introduced for the 1959 competition was that 20 rods from each heat would qualify to fish in the final instead of 10. "Thompson's of Carlow" sponsored a 12ft "plastic" boat for the heaviest fish prize. Among the early entries to the event was the Minister for the Gaeltacht, Mr Micheál Ó Móráin and the American Ambassador Mr Scott McLeod.

A measure of the interest being taken was the conclusion of an agreement between the Castlebar Anglers' Association and the BBC under which the event would be televised for viewing in Great Britain. In an editorial in "The Connaught Telegraph", May 2nd 1959 reference was made to the fact that no mention whatever was made of the big event in an official publication – a brochure especially produced by Bord Fáilte to cover sporting events in 1959, even though particulars of the competition had been sent on to the (American Ambassador Scott McLeod competed at Cushlough in 1959) publishers. The editorial continued " The World Trout Angling Competition – the biggest angling festival of its kind in Europe – is one of the very few competitions in Ireland that has in fact attracted over-seas visitors: It is too, one of the few Tostal attractions which has not been subsidised by the Irish Taxpayer".

The seventh World trout angling competition fished over Whit weekend in 1959 proved to be disappointing from a fishing point of view because of the brilliant sunshine. It attracted a maximum of 192 entries and entries had to be refused because no more boats or boatmen were available. A particular pleasure for the visiting anglers was meeting and receiving a hearty welcome from the club's President and founder member, Mr P. T. Moran. Ninety-four years old and hale and hearty, Mr Moran who was known as the "father of Irish angling" did not compete that year but was present to greet all competitors. Mr Scott McLeod, the American Ambassador did not qualify but was reported to have enjoyed the experience.

*American Ambassador Scott McLeod at Cushlough Bay for 1959 World Cup.*

Micheál Ó Móráin, Minister for the Gaeltacht qualified for the final and was only beaten by a slender margin for a prize. One of the greatest thrills anglers and competitors got during the competition was to hear the announcement that the blind angler, Jack Vincent had qualified in the first heat and won the 2nd overseas prize in the final.

"The greatest thrill of my life was to rise and play a fish as this time last year I thought I would never fish again," said Mr W. Boyle Fawsitt, who was a well-known Dublin solicitor, fishing for the first time since he recovered from serious injuries received in a motor accident on the previous year.

Forty-eight boats took part in the first 2 heats and 21 qualified each day, Brilliant sunshine and dead calm waters made conditions most unsuitable. Despite this the sun baked and blistered competitors returned 54 fish the first day and 56 on the 2nd day. A strong breeze on Monday for the final was a big improvement but the continuous strong sunshine was against ideal fishing conditions. The winner Mr D. Haltom, Coothill, Co Cavan had a catch of eight fish weighing 4lbs 8.5ozs.

*Minister for Gaeltacht, Micheál Ó Móráin presents World Cup to D. Halton, Cootehill and seated, Rev Anthony O'Toole C.C.*

Mr Boyle Fawsitt, Dublin received the 2nd prize with 2 fish weighing 3lbs 11.5ozs and third was Dr E O'Hara with 3 fish weighing 3lbs 3.75ozs.

The prize for the fibreglass boat for the heaviest trout went to Mr A. Foley, Bundoran. The weigh in each evening was under the supervision of Chief Supt H. J. Keegan, Very Rev. Jackson, Tuam, Mr T. Coucill, Secretary, Ms Gus Wynne, P. J. Howard, R. Tarpey, M. Phelan, W. Cameron, W. Lavelle, James McVeigh, Inland Fisheries Trust and J. Bourke, Ballinrobe.

Mr Ó Móráin, Minister for the Gaeltacht speaking at the final dinner stated that he had worked hard but unfortunately he only met three Irish speaking fish and they came from the Tourmakeady side. Two of them were captured and a third got away.

# Chapter 2

## 1960 – 1st and 3rd, Prizes go Overseas

Paddy O'Malley of Tucker Street, Castlebar caught a great trout, probably the best ever caught with fly on Lough Carra during the Mayfly season. I understand that the trout was caught near Church Island to a Rogan Yellow Wing Mayfly and weighed 14lbs 2ozs.

A report in *The Connaught Telegraph* of the 14th May 1960 stated that for the past seven years Lough Mask has had the special attention of the Inland Fisheries Trust, who have removed tens of thousands of pike and perch predators from its waters, with the result that the trout fishing, always outstanding, has improved still further in recent years. For the World Cup (June 4th to 6th) the Mayfly season will be at its best and excellent sport is forecast if the weather is reasonably satisfactory. The Cushlough foreshore where the competition starts and finishes had a face-lift within the past few weeks. With the help of a Bord Fáilte grant the Ballinrobe anglers had made an excellent job of levelling and metalling the foreshore to provide a spacious car park and hard standing for spectators and anglers. Cost of the work was stated to be £725.

Entry fee for the competition remained at £5. An increased number of overseas

*Paddy O'Malley, Tucker St, Castlebar with his trout of 14lbs 2ozs from Lough Carra.*

*From left: Martin Phelan, Dick Tarpey, Revd Dean Jackson, Tom Coucill, Sergearnt H. Glynn and D. Carroll at weigh-in.*

anglers were reported as having participated which gave the event more of an international flavour.

Mr Jack Vincent, the blind angler won Saturday's Heat with one fish weighing 1lb 9ozs. and finished in third place on Monday. Mr Vincent McGovern, Newport won Sunday's Heat with 2 fish weighing 1lb 12:25ozs. Mr R. Phelan with a London address, was the very popular overall winner. Well known in the west Mr Phelan resided in Westport for many years before moving to London and also qualified for the overseas prize. His catch was 5 fish weighing 3lbs 12.75ozs followed by Sydney Costello, Westport 2 fish, 2lbs 7.5ozs and third was Jack Vincent with one fish weighing 1lb 8ozs.

*The Connaught Telegraph* reported that the audacious weatherman was in his most capricious mood, and the total catch of fish over the three days was most disappointing and did not do justice to the fishery. However, for the first time since the inauguration of the event, the World Cup went overseas; so also did the third and fourth prizes and from a tourism point of view this was rightly hailed as a great result for the competition. Records of total catch numbers for the competition are incomplete. Saturday's heat looked like being as low as 18 anglers catching 19 fish weighing 16lbs while Sunday's was 15 anglers with 17 fish weighing 14lbs 4ozs. In the final the first 6 anglers caught 12 trout weighing 11.75lbs.

# 1961 – Angler won Boat, Bride & World Title

Another increase in overseas entries was predicted for the 1961 World Cup and at an early stage and bookings from the UK are reported as brisk. Mr John B. Moran from Denver, Colorado, brother of Micheál Ó Móráin arrived early in Castlebar for the event and announced that he had brought the killing fly with him. There was a growing air of excitement amongst the competitors following an announcement that three new flies named "Grace", "Jacqueline" and "Gagarin" will be opposing each other in the great battle of Lough Mask. *The Connaught Telegraph* reported that expert fly tier Jimmy McHale of Castlebar has added a fourth famous name to the recent new fly creations and it is called "Shepard" after the first U.S. astronaut Commander Alan B. Shepard.

While the success of Al Foley, Dromahair, Co Leitrim, in winning the ninth World Trout Fly competition on Lough Mask on Whit Monday was acclaimed by everyone, it also shows – that he has been favoured with remarkable luck on each of his three visits to Mayo to fish the competition. In 1959, the first year Al fished the competition, he won a fibreglass boat valued at £75. On the occasion of his second visit he met on the shore of Lough Mask, under rather unusual circumstances, the girl who later became his wife and now on his third visit, he had won the World Cup.

The weather during this competition was reported to be excellent for the three days and this was reflected in a good catch. On Saturday 51 of the 92 anglers landed 77 fish weighing 65lbs. The heat winner Dr Eamon Scully, Galway had 6 fish weighing 4lbs 10ozs. Mr B. Gibbons, Westport, won the heat on Sunday with 4 fish weighing 5lbs .25ozs. In the 2nd heat on Sunday 44 of the 92 anglers caught 76 fish weighing 92lbs and in the final 26 of the 43 competitors caught 71 fish weighing 65lbs. This gave a total catch of 224 fish weighing 216lbs, one of the best results since the competition started. Al Foley's winning catch on Monday was no less than 10 trout weighing 10lbs 2.5ozs followed by B. Gibbons, Westport in 2nd place with 10 fish weighing 8lbs .5ozs, and third J. McGowan, Clonmel 3 fish for 4lbs 12ozs.

While fishing in the competition Mr S. J. McCormack joint secretary of Castlebar Mitchells G.A.A. Club hooked a trout of about 1lb. Just as the boatman Mr L. Cameron, Ballinrobe was about to net the fish there was a huge splash and a big pike swallowed the trout, Mr McCormack played the pike for about 20 minutes and just when it seemed he might catch the 2 fish the pike, estimated to weigh about 12lbs, ate through the cast and made off with his meal.

Yet another hard luck story from this competition was the unusual experience of Mr Ernest Everard, Castlebar, Mr Everard landed a trout of about 1lb before lunch, and while lunching on an island with his partner and boatman a seagull dived gracefully down, seized the fish and, after conveying it for 200 yards, dropped it into the lake, following a cry of despair from the startled anglers.

Mr Everard who was Hon Sec. of the Mayo Regional Game Council stated that if the fish had not been snatched on him, he had every chance of qualifying. However the report states that the Game Council had carried out intensive schemes of vermin destruction including that of the black backed gulls, it was generally assumed that the bird was seeking revenge when it robbed Mr Everard of his chance of qualification.

A speech by Micheál Ó Móráin, Minister for Lands and Fisheries dwelt at length with the problems of poaching on a commercial scale, which were on the increase at the time. A new technique of poisoning was being carried out on an organised basis in some areas. The Minister announced that a public enquiry would take place at the Courthouse in Castlebar on 27th June into the desirability of regulating by way of size limit, bag limit or otherwise, trout fishing on the waters in the area which were being developed by the Inland Fisheries Trust. The views of all anglers would be sought. A special presentation of prizes for boatmen was made to Mr John Bourke, J. Prendergast, J. Duffy and B. Murphy. Mr W. Scorer, Westmoreland won the prize for the best overseas angler.

## 1962 – Return to Easter for the Tenth

A review of the first 9 years of the World Cup was carried out and it revealed more information on the circumstances under which the competition got underway and also decided to revert to Easter weekend in 1962 for the 10th competition. The following is an extract from *The Connaught Telegraph* of April 14th 1962. "Ten years ago, when the competition was started in conjunction with An Tostal, it received no encouragement from any source; no financial assistance from the State subsidised bodies who have squandered millions building castles in the air; there was open hostility from the top brass of Irish Angling Councils; there was bitterness and jealousy in county and provincial angling circles. How dare Castlebar or any club in the west of Ireland seek the limelight! We'll deal with this upstart Association that generally was the attitude. Looking back, perhaps the bitter opposition served a useful purpose, for it did succeed in getting the backs of the Angling Association properly up. They became determined to go ahead, to run the gauntlet of their critics. Without a penny piece to credit, but with the good will and co-operation of local people, many of whom never cast a fly, the first World Trout Fishing Competition was launched in 1953 at a cost of

£1,000. In the intervening years the competition had gone from success to success; more important it has achieved what it set out to achieve – it has attracted overseas visitors here; and in doing so it has achieved more for tourism and angling in the West than was ever achieved before. It has given a new lease of life to the boat-building industry here, and brought hope to the despairing and vanishing boatmen of Lough Mask. Further, it has put Mayo and Mask on the angling maps of the world." Following on this there was an appeal from the sponsoring club to all those competitors who pioneered the project to participate once again in celebration of a decade of achievement. Obviously there is no smoke without fire and some opposition to launching of this event in 1953 and its annual staging since then must have existed.

One hundred and seventy-six competitors took part in the 10th annual World Cup Competition in 1962. Once again conditions for fishing were anything but ideal – there was brilliant sunshine, long periods of calm, and an unsettled wind when it did blow, with the result that the catch of fish individually and collectively, was the worst since the great competition began in 1953 and with one notable exception, many of the more famous anglers who had featured in the prizes up to then did not qualify for the final day on that occasion.

The winner was Mr James Cox, a building contractor from Westport with 5 trout weighing 4lbs 8ozs. In second place was Mr H. R. Lawrence of Tullamore with 2 fish, 3lbs 4.75ozs and third was Mr Jack Stack of Westport, probably the most consistent angler of all time participating in the event with 1 fish, 2lbs

*Mícheál Ó Móráin, Minister for Lands and Fisheries presents 1962 World Cup to Jim Cox, Westport.*

11.25ozs. Mr B. Mulcahy, Dungarvan was fourth and Mr Jack Vincent, the blind overseas angler was 5th and won the overseas prize. Miss Vera Browne, Ballinrobe, won the special ladies prize and the heaviest fish prize was won by Dr McDarby from Ballinrobe. The record of Number of fish caught is incomplete, but on Saturday the 20 qualifying rods caught 39 fish weighing 44.3lbs and 19 qualifiers on Sunday caught 26 fish weighing 29.59Ibs.

Once again Mr Micheál Ó Móráin, Minister for Lands & Fisheries presented the prizes to the winners and Martin Phelan, Vice-Chairman of the club presided in the absence of Paddy Howard who was indisposed through illness. The Minister referred to the fact that the trout on Lough Mask must have marked political views as far as he was concerned because he only succeeded in catching one 7oz trout. He referred to the ongoing development work by the Inland Fisheries Trust. After the prizes were presented 97 year old Mr P. T. Moran, President of the Club, was given a great ovation as he expressed the wish that Paddy Howard, who was indisposed, would be back among the anglers on the following year.

The new World Champion James Cox was met at Westport on Easter Monday evening by a cavalcade of cars and accorded a great welcome in the town.

## 1963 – A Cold Start

*The Connaught Telegraph* of the 19th January 1963 reported that residents in the area of Lough Carra continued an ancient sport of their own that of fishing on the ice covered lake. The continuous hard frost since Christmas attracted young and old on to the heavily frozen lake equipped with spears, forks and other lethal weapons. They concentrate on one bay and search until they find a pike. They then give chase and sometimes manage to tire the fish, which is then extracted by breaking the ice. Apparently pike of up to 30lbs weight were taken in January 1963.

Meanwhile the Castlebar Club was once again thinking of the World Cup for that year and once more it was decided to change the competition to Whit Weekend, which fell from the 1st to the 3rd of June on that year. Salmon fishing was reported as excellent in Mayo early that year and expectations were high that a marked improvement would also happen in the trout scene which had been below average in the previous year. Quite a number of parties of English anglers entered to compete in 1963 and Tom Coucill Hon. Sec. of the event since its inauguration revealed that to date over 2,000 anglers had competed. Some difficulty was reported in getting the required number of boats as the entry numbers reached the 200 cut off point.

The competition was gradually surpassing the aims of the promoters in attracting more and more angling visitors to the West, and the most noticeable feature of the success it was attaining in that direction was the fact that apart from the visiting anglers who took part in the competition, it was attracting parties of anglers who came to fish the Western lakes several times each year during the season. The Inland Fisheries Trust supervisor for Lough Mask and Lough Carra, Michael Tolan who had taken up his appointment shortly before the competition was a very popular winner of the 1963 competition with a catch of 4 fish weighing 2 lbs 14.5ozs followed by A. H. Lawrence in 2nd place with 4 fish weighing 2 lbs 4.75ozs and in 3rd, the man who always seemed to feature in a prominent position Jack Stack with 3 fish weighing 2 lbs 4.5ozs. The total catch of 266 fish was the highest on record so far and was exceptional considering that sunshine made conditions unsuitable for fishing each day. On Saturday a total of 107 fish were caught weighing 114 lbs, while on Sunday 86 fish were returned weighing 66 lbs. Many fish under 10 inches were reported as being returned to the water on both days. B. Keaney of Galway won the heat on Saturday with 5 fish weighing 5lbs 1.25ozs. P. O'Loughlin, Ennis won Sunday's heat with 4 fish weighing 3lbs 10.5ozs. A special tribute was paid to Miss Vera Browne, Ballinrobe, who had won the ladies prize once again and also to the Lough Mask boatmen for their wonderful co-operation.

## 1964 – Robbie takes World Cup

M. Ó Móráin, Minister for Lands & Fisheries announced at the World Cup dinner in Castlebar that since the first angling development plan was initiated in 1957 there had been a steady annual rise in income from angling visitors. 1964 however, had recorded a 30% increase over the 1963 figures. He was proud of the progressive role adopted by the Castlebar anglers, not only to fishery development but also the promotion of angling tourism through the World Cup.

The twelfth annual World Cup competition, which took place over Whit weekend, lost none of its former greatness as the prime fishing event for trout on these islands. The competition was held in mixed weather conditions and Lough Mask did not fish very well. The competitors however are reported to have fought every minute of the time allocated to them in a do or die effort to win honours. The result was a neck and neck struggle with half an ounce tipping the scales in favour of popular Ballinrobe angler Robbie O'Grady, and giving him first prize. Robbie caught 3 fish weighing 2lbs 15ozs beating Paddy O'Malley of Castlebar into 2nd place with three fish weighing 2lbs 14.5ozs. Winner of 3rd prize was Jim Telford, Belfast with 3 fish weighing 2lbs 7.5ozs. Last year's champion Michael Tolan was 4th with 4 fish weighing 2lbs 7.5ozs, and a former World Champion Al Foley, now resident in the UK, was the overseas prize-winner with

*Robbie O'Grady, Ballinrobe, receives the 1964 World Cup from Mícheál Ó Móráin, Minister for Lands and Fisheries, with Hon. Sec. Tom Coucill and Chairman Paddy Howard in the background.*

5 fish over the two days weighing 5lbs 14ozs. Mr R. McQuiston, Belfast won the prize for the heaviest fish weighing 2lbs 11.25ozs. Eighty-two anglers weighed in 117 fish on Saturday in ideal weather conditions and the heat winner was John Burns, Ballinrobe with 3 fish weighing 4lbs 1.75ozs. Brilliant sun and a dead flat lake did not contribute to good fishing in the 2nd Heat. Of the 84 anglers only 37 weighed in a total of 63 fish with the heaviest catch going to Luke Higgins of Ballinrobe who had 4 fish weighing 4lbs 4.25ozs.

**The Jack Stack Era**

*The Connaught Telegraph* reported that Jack Stack first started tying flies as a hobby in the late 40s / early 50s. Very quickly the flies became popular and came to the notice of Mons J. Nadaud, editor of the fishing magazine "La Peche et Les Poissons" following a successful angling outing on Lough Mask with Jack. Although a busy chemist in Westport Jack commenced tying flies on a commercial basis, using all the standard patterns of the day and invented the "Grace Kelly", a fly that won him the 1953 World Cup. Jack was placed in most of the early World Cup competitions and had a 2nd and three third places in addition to two heat wins. The Daily Express in an article on April 12th 1962 quoted Jack Stack as saying that his wife gave him a present of a fly tying kit to start him off. His materials – feathers of mallard and pheasants he shot during the winter and cockerels feathers he picked up in farmyards. Another Jack Stack special of the time was the "Connaught Ranger" – it had dark blue dun hackle, seal fur body tied with silver, and finished with mallard wing. Jack tried it out and caught 80 trout with it. In 1962 he introduced it to the World Cup Competition on Easter Saturday and Sunday and went very close to taking his second World Cup Title. He finished that year in 3rd place and it is safe to suggest that both "Grace Kelly" and the "Connaught Ranger" were on his team of flies. Jack fished Mask with great success for many years and I had the pleasure of making his acquaintance while he was fishing with Leo Joyce some years ago. Both of them have now departed this life but there are trout who remember them especially in the Rocky Shore and Ballygarry areas of Lough Mask.

*Jack Stack with a 6 lb 12 oz trout caught on a Golden Olive, Lough Mask 1961.*

## Tom Coucill 1st Hon Secretary of the "World Cup"

As the hard working Secretary of Castlebar & District Anglers Tom Coucill could be described as the driving force behind this competition together with Chairman Paddy Howard. I did not have the pleasure of knowing Tom too well, but my earliest memories of him were passing his scooter by on the road to Gortnor Abbey, Lough Conn each Whit weekend for a number of years. I did fish a Heat of the Lough Conn International Competition many years ago with Larry McNeely as boatman, and Tom as partner, but still did not get to know him too well because we were both quite busy on the same day. On that day the grilse were jumping freely not too far from Gortnor Abbey and Larry, being a lover of Salmon fishing continually urged us to present the flies to the pitching Grilse. Tom insisted that we were in a trout competition but I decided to cover the Grilse, and on three occasions I rose and hooked a trout, much to the amazement of Tom. All I can remember about Tom's fishing that day was he loved fishing in the trough between the waves and drawing in the flies sideways over the bow of the boat which also meant that Larry and myself had to be on our guard as the flies were sometimes, dangerously close. Tom was a Lancashire man, proprietor of the then Humbert Inn in Castlebar and his secretarial skills made a major impact on the angling scene.

Charles Russel of *The Connaught Telegraph* credits him with putting Castlebar on the World's angling map in a very revealing article of April 1964. "Bearded, aesthetic, eccentric, and one of those rare geniuses that emerge now and then in a generation, a brief reference to his many hobbies, interests and pursuits will explain what a versatile and remarkable person he was. A gifted artist, sculptor, taxidermist; a keen numismatist, philatelist, botanist, zoologist, ornithologist, ichthyologist (and there were more) he has identified many species of rare birds, fish and plants submitted to him. A keen angler, he represented Ireland on two occasions and steered the fortunes of the only national event to survive An Tostal. Impatient to the point of aggressiveness, short-tempered, so serious was he that if he smiled one would expect to hear the fracture of a jaw. His concern was 'Get on with the job'. Tom has merited a place on the rostrum in the hall of fame – a special place reserved for those who serve the community for it is on the individual contribution to the community that the worth of the citizen is based. Tom's has been a rich invaluable one".

I reproduce this article on Tom Coucill because I believe that he played a central role in the saga of Ireland's Trout Fly World Cup Competition.

## 1965 – Transfer to Ballinrobe

In the month of March fourteen brown trout averaging 9 lbs were caught on the troll by Dr J. V. McDarby of Ballinrobe on Lough Mask in three outings. The doctor's first outing, lasting two hours, resulted in two massive specimen trout of 15.25 and 12.5lbs – the sort of fish which most anglers hardly see in a lifetime, never mind catch. A week later, using the same copper and silver Punjab spoon he brought in five more for a total weight of 41.5lbs. *The Connaught Telegraph* reports that five days later again, Dr McDarby took the largest capture of all, a further seven trout which sent the scales shooting to 61.5lbs. This must be an all time record, which is unlikely to be surpassed. A pity that more of these monsters would not surface to the fly!

The AGM of the Castlebar Anglers reported a loss of £36 in hosting the 1964 World Cup but the Club decided to continue the World Cup competition during the Whit Weekend of 1965. Two major difficulties however loomed on the horizon. A letter from the secretary of the Ballinrobe Boatmen's Association Mr Jimmy Murphy was read at a further meeting of the Castlebar Club stating that only 30 boats would be available and that there would be some further complications. The further complications arose from the fact that at Whit weekend most if not all available boatmen would be on hire, many to their regular annual customers. One must remember that late May/early June coincided with the peak of the Mayfly season on Lough Mask and unlike today, nearly all angling visitors who came on holidays at the time required the services of a boatman. Prior to 1965, 45 to 52 boats were made available for the competition and the reduced number of boats presented a major problem for hosting the competition. This had not presented the same difficulties for the organisers at Easter, but the harsher weather at that time was causing its own difficulties.

At this time also there was news of an International Competition to be organised for Whit weekend on Lough Conn and this would present further difficulties for the organisers of the Mask event. There were also those who believed that Ballinrobe with its own Angling Club who had purchased the foreshore and boat berthing area at Cushlough in the Forties should be gaining more from the competition. However, as this record is intended to trace the history of the competition and to give credit to the many people who were involved on a voluntary basis both in Castlebar and Ballinrobe in the organisation of this great competition I chose not to pursue in any further detail the circumstances of transfer of the competition administration to Ballinrobe. Suffice to say that a short news item appeared in "The Connaught Telegraph" later in 1965 stating that Ballinrobe anglers were making arrangements to hold a big angling competition on Lough Mask over August weekend. Entries were expected from all over the country and efforts were being made to attract overseas anglers. A further Press release in the *Western People* stated that "Ballinrobe Competitions Committee" were going ahead with arrangements to replace the abandoned World Trout Angling Competition on Lough Mask on Saturday and Sunday, July 31st, August 1st with the Final on the Bank Holiday Monday August 2nd and the town traders organisation had sponsored a silver challenge cup for the first prize winner.

President of the committee was Rev Monsignor Gunnigan; Chairman, Dr J.J. Cummins; Vice-Chairman, Thos Guckian; Secretary, Raymond Ansboro; Treasurer, Michael Tolan; assistant secretaries, Paddy Varley, Jimmy Murphy, Boat managers, Thomas Duffy, Tom Cusack; Committee: Michael Curtin, Rev Bro. Cooke, Dr McDarby, Thomas Varley, Thomas Dunleavy, Edwin Finlay, Robert O'Grady, Henry Murphy, Luke Higgins, Tony Mulloy, John Burns, and William Gibbons.

Approaching August weekend reports from Lough Mask seemed very favourable with John Joe Malone catching 14 in one outing, while Miss Vera Browne and Mrs M. Walsh landed 12 in another outing. (Heaviest being 4lbs).

The trout were not rising as freely on the final Monday of the inaugural competition under Ballinrobe administration. The *Western People* reports that of the 40 anglers who qualified for the final only 17 weighed in fish with a total of 29 trout weighing 30 lbs 7ozs. Total catch for the three-day event in which 136 anglers competed was 198 trout, weighing 208lbs. 7ozs. First prize of 150 pounds and the Waterford Cutglass Trophy, presented by Ms A. Guinness went to Frank Smyth, still a very regular visitor to the area with a winning catch of 3 fish for 6lbs 3ozs.

In second place was local man John Joe Malone with 3 fish for 3lbs 14ozs and third was D McCarthy, Cork with 2 fish weighing 2lbs -0.5ozs. Martin Phelan, Castlebar, won heaviest fish prize with a fish of 4lbs 3ozs and best lady angler once again was Miss Vera Browne, Ballinrobe.

Mr Micheál Ó Móráin, Minister for Lands, presented the prizes and congratulated the organizers on the success of their first effort. The Minister hoped that fishermen throughout Ireland would co-operate in making a success of this competition. Rev. C. Langan Vice-President of the Committee referred to the great work being done by the I.F.T. on the rivers and lakes in the area. Mr Luke Higgins presented his perpetual cup for the heaviest fish of the competition to Martin Phelan. Secretary, Raymond Ansboro was thanked for his input to the competition.

I am reliably informed that it was only at this stage that outboard engines were used for the competition. Prior to this, although some boatmen had outboard engines, in order to preserve a level playing pitch they did not use them in the competition. Nowadays one can only marvel at the boatmen of Lough Mask and other large Irish lakes for the magnitude of their task, especially when faced with strong winds. The relative comforts provided by the outboard engines of today are so great that we can only guess at what "braving the elements" meant in those days. The change-over was not without its dangers. Many of the narrow "rowing friendly" boats at the time did not have the strong transoms of today and it was not unusual for a boat to spring a leak around the transom while using the engine. This happened mainly with the heavier engines which were not very plentiful. The "Seagull"outboard engine of 2.5 to 3.5HP would be the most popular and still a far cry from the 10Hp and 15HP that are commonplace today. One of my earliest memories of the competition is that of John, a tall boatman from Cahir refusing the request of one of his competitors to use a 10HP Mercury provided by the competitor instead of his own Seagull. John was probably more aware of the likely dangers of this practise and wisely opted for the steady progress of his seagull engine.

# 1966 – Munster Winner for the 1st time

Tom Cameron stalled the oars on Lough Mask and told George Burrows the story of the two pennies and the grasping fairies. Tom had been with an English angler, the sporting military type, who was doing no good at the fishing – this happened a few years ago. It was not that the angler was a novice; he wasn't indeed; he had fine tackle and a lot of patience, but he could not catch fish, although others were getting them. After the 21st day the sore and tired angler said that the Lough Mask fairies were to blame; they wanted money and they would

*Dick Willis, Bridge Bar, Mallow, Co. Cork – first Munster winner of World Cup 1966.*

not give him fish until they got cash. So the angler was rowed to an island. He took two pennies from his pocket and using a lump of limestone, he hammered the two coins into the bark of a tree. All this was known to Tom. It was then evening, so angling was adjourned until next morning. In the interval Tom, while taking in some liquid, met a Ballinrobe townsman who listened intently to the story. "I'll carry that a bit further," says he; "where's that tree with the pennies in it?" Tom gave detailed description, and next morning went as usual to collect the English angler. This morning Tom did an unusual thing; he suggested a certain fly to the angler; something he had not done before because the angler did not want it that way; he wanted to use only his own selection. The Englishman (they are very innocent these English) began to catch whopping big trout. It was almost magical, as though Tom and the fairies had conspired somewhere near Tourmakeady in the night to delight the Englishman. When 5 or 6 fine trout were captured Tom and his charge found themselves in the boat near the island of the pennies and the Englishman insisted on going ashore to see what had happened to the pennies. They had gone! Removed during the night by the mercenary fairies, who now because they had got the "dough" were giving trout for all they were worth! The Englishman believed it, too.

George was on Lough Mask with Tom Cameron during the World Cup that year and was so keen to catch fish that he suggested to Tom that he would hammer two half crowns into a tree (the stakes were high after all) they were fishing for a prize of £150, a Guinness Waterford bowl and a Town Traders' Cup that was as big as anything that came out of Texas, but Tom would have none of it; the fairies would stay inactive for August bank holiday. The Ballinrobe committee was now running the competition George was writing about. George suggests that the fairies may have turned against the Castlebar men – or maybe it was the Mask boatmen? – but now the Ballinrobe men organise their own contest. The emphasis is very much, and very properly, on Ballinrobe. It is a friendly town that has time, indeed makes time, to think of sport and good companionship. Anyone who had the idea that the competitors he met during the event were money grabbers, angling with aggressive intensity to gain a couple of pounds would be entirely wrong. They fished keenly, that is true, and many of them fished skilfully, but after that they sang songs and told stories and supported breweries.

George continues : "The Ballinrobe organisers, including Raymond Ansboro, Hon. Secretary, and Anthony McCormack, Hon. Treasurer, stressed to me that the group don't want to make money out of the competition, but they do want to do something for Ballinrobe". "They have gained a good access road to the lake at Cushlough Bay, which has the familiar long slender weeds that grow through the clear water; that is where the trout live and can be caught, without going out into the lake proper (should you wish to stay) but on sunny days it might be just as well to hammer a few coins into an adjacent alder tree!!"

Those among us who follow soccer will remember the success of England in the Soccer World Cup in 1966, but Ballinrobe were getting ready to ensure the success of another World Cup. The Ballinrobe Competitions Committee took their brief extremely seriously from the start and decided to circularise local business people with a view to enlisting their support, and the response was reported to have been excellent.

Angling reports this year mention Mr N. Hewetson and his son Norman landed 22 trout averaging llb 8ozs to the fly in one outing. Mr Michael Horan, Derrymore and Mr Pat O'Connell, Westport landed 18 averaging llb 8ozs including a 3lbs 8oz and a 3lb trout. Dick Willis from Mallow arrived in good time to see England win the World Cup soccer final on TV in the Valkenburg Hotel. However, he recalled that he had forgotten to book accommodation and because of the competition, all-available beds were booked out. However, Tony Mulloy came to his rescue and got him accommodation in the home of the late Mrs McGooey, New Street. Dick prepared to fish his heat of the competition the next day and what a competition he had ? Competition Secretary, Raymond Ansboro reported brisk business and a total of 122 anglers competed for prizes of increased value. The Ballinrobe Traders presented a Silver Cup for the 1st prize-winner and the

Ballinrobe & District Anglers presented a Silver Challenge Cup for the best competing Lady angler. Cash prizes were also increased.

Rough and squally weather conditions did not make fishing ideal for the competition. Dick Willis informs me that he fished the Sunday heat that year and won with a catch of 7 trout weighing 7.5lbs. Of the 122 anglers who finally fished the competition only 67 weighed in and their total catch was 118 trout. The all-out winner on the next day was the same Dick Willis, who is also a well known Irish international angler. Dick had a catch of 5 trout weighing 4lbs .75ozs and his partner in the boat was Dr McDarby, Ballinrobe with Patrick Finnerty as the winning boatman. The winning fish were caught in the Canal area and the winning flies were size 10 Golden Olive and Bibio. I would hazard a guess that celebrations took place in the "Bridge Bar" Mallow, well into the night. Dick Willis was the first Lough Mask World Cup winner from Munster. 2nd place went to Tom Varley, Ballinrobe with one fish weighing 3lbs 1.25ozs and 3rd was Jim O'Connor, Castlebar with 2 trout weighing 2lbs 12.5ozs. Heaviest Fish Prize went to Miss Vera Browne, Ballinrobe and weighed 3lbs 11.5ozs. Dr Jimmy Cummins presided at the dinner in the Valkenburg Hotel that night and Mr G. Burrows, Irish Times, presented the winners with their prizes. Winning Boatmen, 1st P. Finnerty, Cloonliffen, 2nd V. Horan, Ballygarry and 3rd J.J. Malone, Kilkeeran, were also presented with their prizes. Other speakers included Mr J. Wardrop, Scotland who thanked the people of Ballinrobe for their kindness to himself and his wife and Mr R. McQuinston, Lisburn, NI. The Chairman paid a special tribute to Secretary Raymond Ansboro for his organisation and devotion to the cause.

## 1967 – Tony Mulloy as Secretary

Angling reports for Lough Mask on this year were quite encouraging and several good catches were reported. Local angler Paddy Varley reported a catch of 4 trout weighing 13.25lbs. 1967 World Cup dates were set for 5th, 6th and 7th of August and newly elected secretary Tony Mulloy reported a number of entries from clubs in England and Scotland at an early date. Recommendations that Lough Carra be preserved as a sanctuary for wild life were backed by the local Gun Club as concern was expressed at the indiscriminate shooting of wild duck in particular on Mask and Corrib. Later this came to pass and the same status was extended to Lough Mask. A Wild Life Research Project was established at the nearby "An Foras Talúntais Research Station" at Creagh. The Minister for Lands, Mr Ó Móráin was present for the launching of the project a few years later and the major part of the evenings' events was the ceremonial release of a few Mallard Ducks who were taken from the Phoenix Park in Dublin for the occasion. However, they must have had no wish to "quack" over South Mayo with Dublin accents, for just as they were released the ducks flew back from whence they came.

A prize fund of £450 was established for the World Cup and once more the Guinness sponsored Waterford Cut Glass Trophy would be available for the winner. One hundred and forty anglers participated in the three day World Cup Competition and 40 qualifiers battled it out for honours on the Bank Holiday Monday. August week-end, although not an ideal fishing time of the year was now becoming firmly established as World Cup week-end. Indeed this suited the local boating situation because as already mentioned many of the local boatmen had their own clients over the earlier Whit week-end, and indeed a good hatch of Mayfly in early June could result in an overkill of fish for the competition. This was not likely to happen in August.

In this particular competition 121 trout were caught over the 3 days and the Minister for Lands, Micheál Ó Móráin presented the prizes to the winners in the Railway Hotel, Ballinrobe at which the Chairman Dr Jimmy Cummins presided. Weather during the first two heats on Saturday and Sunday was not ideal for fishing. Strong gales and drizzling rain did not contribute to good catches and of the 60 anglers that took part in Saturday's heat, only 28 competitors weighed in fish. The decision of the Committee not to weigh in fish under 12 inches in length was reflected in the number of trout presented for weigh-in and the "Western People" reported that many anglers felt that 10 inch trout which was the legal limit at the time should have been permitted as in former years. The extension of the limit was introduced as a conservation measure at that time and was later to be introduced by the Galway Board of Conservators as a statutory requirement for the Corrib system.

The overall winner who collected a cheque for £150 with the Guinness Cut Glass Trophy and the Ballinrobe Traders Cup was Mr T. Meharg, Belfast and the winning catch was 3 fish weighing 4lbs 2.5ozs. 2nd prize of £50 went to Pat O'Connell of Westport for 2 trout weighing 2lbs 7ozs. In third place was Mr J. Wardrop, Scotland with 2 fish weighing 2lbs 6.75ozs and the Heaviest Fish Prize, the Luke Higgins Cup and £25 added went to Jim O'Connell, Westport, with a trout weighing 3lbs 10ozs. The best boatman was Tom Cusack, Cushlough and Willie Murphy, Cahir also won a boatman's prize.

**Carraigín Dá Bhó**

As spare boatman, Tom Cameron entertained George Burrows once more to a day on the Mask. George described the Partry Mountains as having a real Gaeltacht blue that flowed out onto the water and around the islands. A slender round tower of smoke rose up from Tourmakeady untroubled by any breeze and when a second smoke tower started to grow Tom suggested that a second citizen of Tourmakeady had just lit his pipe! That was the kind of day it was. Almost useless for fishing but still a good day to be out! Tom related the story of the Island of the Two Cows (Carraigín Dá Bhó) for George. A farmer owned this island, which had enough grazing for two cows. They were put out there and the farmer promised his wife that he would row across each day to see to the cows. The husband, however was more interested in going down to the pub each evening. All he did was go to a point on the mainland and look over at the island. He saw each day what he believed were the outlines of two cows and off he went to the pub. Six months later when he really went across, he found the cows very dead indeed; the outlines had been two rocks! Today in the district when a mother tells her "courting" son to go and look at the cows he is more interested in grasping the physical outline of his girl and so, he gives merely a glance at the livestock. That glance was adopted as a local description which immortalises the story of the man and the two island cows.

## 1968 – To Westport once again

Following a Committee meeting held in May of that year the announcement was made that the World Cup/ August Weekend Festival would only have 50 Boatmen available. The explanation given was that the decision was to ensure that in the interests of safety, all anglers would be accompanied by a fully qualified Boatman. However, this also had the effect of limiting entries to 100 anglers which was somewhat less than the numbers competing heretofore.

The Connacht Cup competition was fished on Lough Mask in early June of that year with 42 anglers weighing in only 20 trout for 22.5lbs. Pat O'Connell, Westport won the competition with 2 fish weighing 2lbs -11ozs and Leo Joyce of Westport came 2nd. It was destined to be a good year for the winner, however.

The Lough Mask Boatmen's Association held their own competition in fine conditions later in July of that year and 35 anglers weighed in 22 fish only, amidst some controversy about the rule debarring fish under 12 inches from the weigh-in. The legal limit at this stage was 10 inches, and many felt that because a large number of fish were taken over 11 inches the result could be somewhat different. This was a boat competition, (2 anglers per boat only) and the winners were John Burns and Tom Dunleavy of Ballinrobe who had 3 fish weighing 5lbs 11.5ozs.

On the week before the competition the local Boatmen's Association guaranteed thirty boats each day so this enabled 120 anglers to compete. The Competition Secretary, Tony Mulloy announced that Germany, France, UK and the USA would be represented at this competition and once more the Committee imposed 12 inch limit would apply.

The weather on each day of the competition was anything but favourable as brilliant sunshine and a "flat" lake kept the trout down, but the final was fished during thunder, lightening and torrential rain.

The overall winner was Mr Pat O'Connell, Westport, who continued the Westport dominance of this event with a catch of 2 fish weighing a modest 2lbs 7.5ozs. Pat received the Ballinrobe Traders Cup and the Waterford Glass engraved Trophy with a cheque for £150 added and was also winner of his Heat on Saturday. John Jennings, Ballinrobe was in 2nd place with 3 fish weighing 2lbs 6.75ozs followed in third place by Michael Tolan, Crossmolina with 2 fish for 2lbs 2.5ozs. The Cup presented by Luke Higgins for the Heaviest Fish went to J. O'Mahony of Ennis and Overseas Prize winner was Dr O'Keeffe of London. The best Lady Angler for the second year in succession was Mrs P. O'Connell, wife of the Winner. Winning Boatmen were: 1, Paddy Varley; 2, J. O'Sullivan; 3. R. O'Grady.

Dr Jimmy Cummins, Chairman of the Committee, presided at the dinner on Monday night and after congratulating the winners he referred to the important role played by fishing in Ballinrobe. Mr George Burrows who presented the prizes said that Ballinrobe had much to offer the tourist- excellent fishing and the friendliest people in the World. The President of the Committee Mons.G. Mitchell expressed the hope that the potential of the area would be considerably developed during the next few years. Mr G. Wardrop, Scotland presented Jimmy Murphy with a prize for the Boatman with the Heaviest Fish Winner. Saturday – 43 fish weighing 39lbs 4ozs, Sunday – 20 fish weighing 16lbs 7.5ozs. On the final day 8 anglers from a qualifying number of 36 weighed in 12 fish weighing 11lbs 9.5ozs. This would be regarded today as a very low average weight for a 12 inch limit weigh in.

## 1969 – Cup to Northern Ireland for 2nd time

Two English anglers returned from a holiday in the Republic with horrific tales of sighting a "Monster" in Lough Carra. In a letter to the editor of a London evening newspaper the two men, Eric Herbert and Philip Simmonds of South West London reported that during an evening fishing expedition on the lake they heard "a sudden swishing noise, and a horrifying monster of some kind thrust its head above the water". It was reported as having a snout like a pig, eyes like a deer, a head like a snake or eel, and a long neck like a giraffe. " 20 yards behind it appeared the all important but unmistakeable hump, the same colour as the head and neck, scaly, dark brown. They were at the time, thirty yards from the "monster", only 50 yards from the shore, but too petrified to move. "After 5 minutes or so" the letter continued, "the monster submerged, the hump slowly disappearing first, followed by the neck and finally the head." They then reported rowing like madmen to the shore, leaving their fishing tackle in the water. Further astonishment, however awaited them on reaching land. They noticed two locals who had been watching them. Had they seen the "monster"? "Yes, of course they had" they said. It had been around for four years and was reputed to have eaten most of the trout in the lake. "Hadn't anyone reported the monster"? they asked in disbelief. "Plenty" they replied, adding wistfully, "but we're Irish and who would believe us?" The letter concluded; "Here are two startled Englishmen who believe them."

Under the "Ballinrobe notes" in the *Western People* a few weeks later a story appeared which we all assume is unlinked; As part of the re-stocking of the Western Lakes with trout, over 50,000 fingerlings were released into Lough Carra from the Inland Fisheries' Trust Hatchery at Clooncrin. The operation was supervised by Mr B. O'Shea, Superintendent, IFT. According to the *Western People* Secretary Tony Mulloy expressed his confidence that the 1969 Festival would excel previous ones. "We have everything that is necessary for a successful competition . . . that is except weather conditions of course, and if we had any say in that direction, we'd arrange for that too." said Tony.

It is unfortunate that of all the competitions I have covered so far there are very scant details of this competition. Suffice to say that the winner of the competition was Jim Telford of Antrim with a catch of 7 trout weighing 6lbs 1oz. George Burrows noticed that, despite the fact that the "Green Peter he was using that day was refused persistently, Jim Telford's Green Peter attracted the winning catch of 7 trout. George also noticed that the tying of the winning fly was quite different from anything around Ballinrobe, or Dublin for that matter. It appeared both smaller and neater with more spectacular colour in the feathers, something trout could hardly resist. In second place came Dr D. O'Keeffe, Eltham, London with 4 trout weighing 4lbs 7.5ozs and third was local Committee member Jimmy Murphy with 5 trout for 3lbs 10.25ozs. H. S. O'Connor, Fermanagh, was the Heaviest Fish prize winner and the winning boatman was P. Feeney, Aughnish, 2nd was W. Murphy, Cahir and third was Robbie O'Grady. M. Horan, Derrymore and Vincent Horan, Ballygarry, in whose boats were the Heat Winners won a pair of oars each presented by John P. Burke, Boatbuilder, Cloonkeary. Dr. Jimmy Cummins presided at the presentation of prizes in the Railway Hotel and Mr. S. C. McMorrow, Secretary of the Inland Fishery Trust, congratulated the winners and appealed for more members of the I.F.T. Michael Heverin, Ireland West, promised more angling development at Cushlough and Cahir. 150 anglers competed and weighed-in 169 trout in 194 rod days.

# Chapter 3

## 1970 – The Boatman is late

A report in the *Western People* of July 1970 noted that Lough Carra, like other Mayo lakes was fishing particularly well. Joe Conroy reported 5 trout averaging 2lbs, Michael Horan, Partry got 4 good trout in one outing, one of which weighed 5lbs 2 ozs and Denis Kelleher, Ballinrobe for 6 trout averaging 1.5lbs. A Dr Heeney and Pete Burke reported 23 trout averaging 1.75lbs in three days fishing.

In spite of an overall decrease in the number of tourists throughout the country, hoteliers and guesthouse owners in Ballinrobe stated that it was business as usual. Many of the proprietors had advance bookings from England, all attracted by the fishing available locally. Another report in July recorded that a German visitor, Mr Meyer with John Joe Malone caught a 13lb trout from Lough Mask. A Dublin Angler, P. Foyle with boatman Paddy Varley landed no fewer than 50 trout averaging 1.5lbs.

On 18th of July James G. Wardrop, Cumnock, Ayrshire, presented Tony Mulloy, Hon. Sec., with a Perpetual Silver Cup which would be on offer for the best competing member of the Lough Mask Boatmen's Association.

August 1st, 2nd and 3rd were designated as World Cup Competition dates. However, heavy skies with little or no breeze did not contribute to good fishing. One regular competitor told the *Western People* reporter that the Lake was teeming with small trout. In spite of this some fine trout were caught including several two pounders and one weighing 3lbs 14ozs. Mr W. McConville, Tandragee, Co. Armagh won the competition with a catch of two trout weighing 5lbs 12.75ozs. Unfortunately, Mr McConville and his brother drowned tragically while swimming in Lough Lannagh, Castlebar some years later during a fishing expedition. In 2nd place that year was well known angler and angling administrator, Vinnie O'Reilly from Headford who had 4 trout weighing 3lbs 6.25ozs and 3rd was Mr E. Murphy of Kinlough, Co. Leitrim with one trout weighing 3lbs 4.5ozs. Dr E. O'Keeffe of Wareham, Dorset got the prize of £50 for the best overseas rod with 3 trout weighing 4lbs 11ozs. He was also awarded the prize for the heaviest fish at 3lbs 8.5 ozs. The Ladies prize, a Silver Perpetual Cup presented by Ballinrobe and District Anglers' Club went to Miss C. Cameron, Ballinrobe and Paddy Varley, Ballinrobe won the Boatmans' prize. In the first heat however, 50 anglers caught 107 trout weighing 98.25lbs and in the 2nd heat 39 anglers caught 76 trout weighing 68.59lbs. In the final 41 anglers weighed in 41 trout weighing 45.48lbs and a record number of 211 anglers competed in the event.

Over the years a set of rules governing the administration of the World Cup Competition evolved, and as various incidents occurred, if the rules were found wanting adjustments were made. This meant that most if not all eventualities were pretty well covered in the rule book, a copy of which was included with each brochure.

I began my Lough Mask boating career for the World Cup Competition in 1970 and one of my first assignments was to act as Boatman for Committee Chairman, Dr Jimmy Cummins and Dr Scully from Oughterard. I had begun my fishing on Lough Mask shortly before this, but had concentrated on the Lively Bay/Rocky Shore area where I had sufficient success. However the good Doctors wanted to proceed to Inishard and the Canal area with all haste. I was happy with my new 4HP McCullough Outboard Engine purchased from the late John Joe Duffy of Kilmaine, also a committee member for the princely sum of £76 and had a new timber boat manufactured by Burke Boats, our local Boat Builder.

*Weighing steward Joe Cusack "measuring up".*

I advised the Chairman of my limitations regarding the Inishard area and set sail for the area in question, comfortable with the knowledge that I had in my possession a number of shearpins if the worst happened. Indeed, as we neared our destination I took one short-cut too many and made contact with one of the many rocks I was later to find out were all too frequent in this area and a shearpin had to be replaced before further progress was made. The day materialised into a competition between the two Doctors and trout were rising in the area, although not that easy to attract. At an early stage Dr Scully established a lead although Dr Cummins also succeeded in getting a fish. At about 3 PM a good rise of trout commenced and we had some feverish activity changing flies and trying to come up with the winning team. At 4 PM Dr Scully had four trout and Dr Cummins had one. Shortly afterwards I asked if it was not time to move closer to home base, knowing that the McCullough Engine while extremely reliable would not break the sound barrier on the way home because of the limitations of a 4HP.

"Ahem, Ahem, we will have time for another try! Just a short drift", said Dr Cummins.

Another drift and two more fish later, one to each angler, we started for home. We arrived into Cushlough Bay at 4 minutes past 6 and hoped that no one noticed us. Alas! The loud hailer with the unmistakeable voice of Tony Mulloy announced that boat no.26 was disqualified and we had a red faced Chairman and a Boatman who had to eat humble pie. I felt sorry for Dr Scully whose catch would have easily qualified him for the final, but resolved in the future to make my own decisions re destinations and departure time. One of the main stories in downtown Ballinrobe that night and for some nights after was about a certain Boatman and a certain Chairman, and it took some time to recover ones pride after the incident.

The competitions carried on although as yet there was no appreciable increase in the numbers competing and much talk at this time of a demand for increases in Boatmen's wages. All sides were keenly aware that it would be only too easy to derail the competition and some compromise on each side of the argument insured that the World Cup competition would persevere. Meetings were held with the Tourist Board to investigate ways of putting the competition on sounder footing and more publicity was sought, but, just as it had started without any outside help back in 1953, so it was destined to continue.

## Changes Herald 1971 World Cup

Committee members for the 1971 World Cup Competition were as follows: Chairman – Dr J. Cummins; Vice-Chairman – Tom Varley; Treasurer – Atty McCormack; Secretary – Tony Mulloy; Boatmanager – R. O'Grady. Committee: J. Murphy, P. Varley, L. Higgins, B. O'Shea, (replaced by Billy Murphy later that year) T. Flanagan, J.J. Duffy, M. Moran, J. Cusack, C. O'Loughlin and D. Kelleher.

Major changes introduced to the competition were as follows. The 1971 World Cup would be extended to take in a third heat and as a result would now commence on the Friday morning with Heat no 1 and would facilitate more anglers as a result. Another change introduced was a team prize. This event would be open to all competitors who decide to fish as a team and the team with the heaviest catch would receive £50 presented by Mr W. P. O'Loghlen, Manager West, Bank of Ireland Group who also offered a further £10 to the best individual angler on any of the participating teams. Team prizes were to be allocated over Heat Weights only.

Secretary, Tony Mulloy reported brisk business and 100 entries were received early in July. Two excellent catches were recorded from the River Robe in mid July. Mr Ronald Webster from Sheffield, who was a regular visitor at this time and an excellent Dry Fly Angler caught a trout of 8.25lbs on the Robe near the entrance to Lough Mask and Mr J. Walsh, High Street, reported catching three fish weighing 9lbs at the same time.

Mr Charles Mitchell, long time chief newsreader with RTE opened a Trout Festival that was organised locally to coincide with the competition. A total of 198 anglers competed in the 1971 World Cup. One hundred and one of these weighed in 183 fish over the Heats. Sixty eight rods qualified to fish the final and of these, 32 weighed in 39 trout, making a total of 222 fish over the four days. Mr Dermot Treacy of Sligo was the World Cup Winner with a final day catch of 2 trout weighing 2lbs 14.75ozs. Dermot was also on the winning team with G. Butler, Sligo, P.J. Brennan, Claremorris and Jimmy O'Reilly, Castlebar. In second place was local committee member Christy O'Loughlin who had 2 trout weighing 2lbs 1.5ozs with Dubliner D.J. Elliot, Dublin, 2 fish 2lbs 1.25ozs in third place. Mrs P. O'Connell, Westport won the Ladies prize Perpetual Cup. Mr M. Matson, London won the overseas prize and the "Heaviest Fish Prize", a perpetual silver cup presented by Luke Higgins, was won by local man Tom Cameron with a trout of 2 lbs 14.5ozs.

## 1972 – New Jetties at Cushlough

Facilities at Cushlough Bay were upgraded early in the year when, as a result of a Bord Fáilte grant Mayo Co. Council erected jetties to facilitate berthing of boats along the shoreline.

Competition dates were set as the 4th to 7th of August inclusive and Dermot O'Connor of the "Market House Tavern" presented sponsorship towards the Boatmens' prize fund. John P. Burke advised the committee that he would like to present a pair of oars and a spinning rod to the committee as prizes and this was to continue and become generous sponsorship from Burke Boats Ltd. Ballinrobe, to the present time. The competition was considered to be the most successful to date in terms of fish caught.

George Allister of Lisburn won the World Cup Trout Wet-Fly competition with a catch of 6 trout weighing 7lbs 1oz, collecting the first prize of the Guinness Trophy, the Ballinrobe Traders' Cup and £150. Local man John Maye came 2nd

*1972 – A group of anglers representing Bank of Ireland in the World Cup Competition. Bill Finn, Roscommon and Larry Scott, Castlebar, display a trout of 6lbs. 3ozs. caught by J. K. O'Riordan, Headford.*

with 4 fish weighing 6lbs 1.5ozs followed in third place by John Jennings with 3 fish weighing 5lbs 15ozs. J.K. O'Riordan, a retired banker from Headford, Co Galway won the Luke Higgins Cup for the heaviest fish with a trout of 6lbs 3ozs caught on the Saturday Heat. Joe Leonard from Southampton won the Overseas' Prize and the ladies Prize (Ballinrobe Anglers' Perpetual Cup) was won by Miss Caroline O'Keeffe. The Bank of Ireland sponsored Team Prize was won by Christy O'Loughlin, Peter O'Malley, Joe Conroy and Denis Kelleher. Heat Winners were as follows; Friday: Christy O'Loughlin 8 Fish weighing 7lbs 5.75ozs; Saturday: Mike Sweeney, Loughrea 9 fish weighing 9lbs 5ozs.; Sunday: P. Doyle 5 fish weighing 5lbs 15.5 ozs. A total of 180 competitors (a slight decrease on the 1971 entry) caught 370 trout weighing 382lbs 14.75ozs and in the final 62 anglers caught 95 trout weighing 123lbs.

The competition lost money however and increasing costs were to plunge the organising committee into a financial crisis and cast some doubt over the status of the event for 1973. The Northern "Troubles" were also having a negative impact on cross border tourism numbers as the World Cup competition had previously recruited approximately one third of its total entry from Northern Ireland.

## Local Committee member and International Angler wins 1973 World Cup

Entries for the World Cup Competition of 1973 closed at an all time record number of 262 competitors and a sum of £100 was added to the first prize cash of £150. Mr John Joe Duffy of Kilmaine, a member of the organising committee and also a member of the Irish International Team since 1970 won the competition and collected the Ballinrobe Traders Cup, Guinness Glass Trophy and a cheque for £250 in highly adverse weather conditions with a catch of 7 trout weighing 8lbs 8.5ozs.

*J. J. Duffy, Kilmaine, Cup Winner 1974.*

John Joe Duffy as a committee member made his own unique contribution to the competition and served as chairman on two occasions. He was captain of the Irish International team in 1974 and will be remembered for a long time for his role in organising the Irish Disabled Anglers' Team and organising competitions at International and National level for the Disabled Anglers.

John Joe was also Secretary of the Connacht Angling Council for many years and it is particularly pleasing to me that someone who had accomplished much for the betterment of angling and who had helped to introduce it to a wider audience

*Audience at 1974 "weigh-in". New boat jetties can be seen in background.*

succeeded in a major competition. In second place was Brendan Costello, Ballinrobe, with 6 fish weighing 7lbs 11.5ozs and third, Denis Kelleher also of Ballinrobe with 5 fish weighing 6lbs 0.5ozs. Winner of the Luke Higgins Cup for the heaviest fish caught went to Cyril O'Donnell of Cork with a fish of 4lbs 11ozs. Mrs Maureen Lyons of Dublin won the Ladies Cup presented by Ballinrobe and District Anglers and Mr Joe Leonard of Southampton won the overseas prize. A total of 262 anglers caught 307 trout weighing 329lbs 10.25ozs. in 327 rod days.

## 1974 – 12 inch Limit is Official

The A.G.M. of 1974 put a committee in place for that year but due to financial difficulties postponed a decision on whether they would proceed with the competition. Thanks to the negotiating skills of the Secretary, Tony Mulloy and the Treasurer, Atty McCormack who had jelled together to make a great team, a once off grant in aid of £150 was made available from Ireland West and a more moderate increase in Boatmans' wages to £5.50 was agreed. Following a meeting held in May and chaired by Dr Cummins the decision was made to go ahead with a competition in 1974.

At the AGM of the World Cup committee a vote of sympathy was proposed

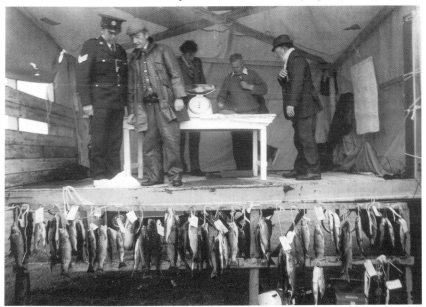

*Sergeant Des O'Kelly; Dr. H. Cummins, Chairman; Michael Tolan; Tony Mulloy, Secretary; and John Joe Duffy at the 1974 weigh-in.*

to the widow of Tom Varley, who was a valued committee member and died at this time.

Following a letter from Ballinrobe & District Trout Anglers requesting that the 10 inch limit for trout be adjusted to 12 inches on Lough Mask, and a debate among the other clubs, the Galway Board of Conservators made an order extending this new limit to Carra, Mask and Corrib.

Ballinrobe Town Traders stated that business was not at all brisk, and attributed this loss to the disturbed state of the North coupled with high charges for air fares and self-drive cars. Reports in the *Western People* commented on the small number of tourists compared with previous years.

The value of the total prize fund for the 1974 World Cup was increased to £700 and a slight decrease over the previous year to 223 anglers entered to compete. The competition was won by Mr Tom Rice, Dublin with 4 fish weighing 8lbs 8ozs. In 2nd place was Ned Murphy, Kinlough, Co Leitrim with 4 weighing 6lbs 4.5ozs and Billy Murphy, Western Regional Fisheries Board was 3rd with 4 trout weighing 5lbs 10.5ozs. Tom Mahon, Sligo had the heaviest single trout with a catch weighing 5lbs 8ozs. Barry Hinde from Cheshire won the Overseas Prize and Mrs Kentgens, Oughterard won the Ladies Prize and the main Boatmans' Prize was won by J.Sullivan. Overall statistics for this year read as follows: A total of 223 rods caught 214 trout weighing 272.75lbs in 279 rod-days.

## 1975 – World Cup for Dublin

The PRO for the World Cup Competition, John P Burke announced that the 23rd World Cup would have a total of £700 in prize money. The winner would also receive a piece of Galway Crystal Cut Glass. Four days of brilliant sunshine and a dead flat lake kept the trout down . The *Western People* reported that 181 competitors "flogged" the lake for miles around during the Heats but failed to entice many fish. 1st Prize went to Mr Pat Doheny, Rathgar Ave, Dublin with 3 trout weighing 5lbs 12ozs. Pat reports that he fished with George Burrows on the final day and that although there was no breeze for most of the day, he was lucky enough to pick a fish in the Shindilla islands area early in the day. Boatman Jimmy Murphy then took his anglers right back to a reef outside Cushlough bay which was not regularly fished. When they arrived there a small but significantly helpful ripple had become established and Pat commenced fishing. Within an hour he had added 2 more trout to his catch and was working hard. He then hooked a good trout of about 2.5lbs and after a short battle the fish got away. Pat states that he remembered seeing money blowing around the boat but then it vanished. He did not realise that at that stage he had the winning catch anyway and attributes his success to the great skill of his boatman Jimmy Murphy.

The 2nd heaviest catch went to Mrs Kentgens, Oughterard, with 2 trout weighing 3lbs 8.5ozs to a "Raymond," who also won the Ladies Challenge Cup presented by the Club and Galway Crystal presented by Mrs J. Moran, Lakeland Hotel. The third prize went to Sean McIntyre, Cavan with 2 fish weighing 3lbs 1oz. Other placings of the final day were in the following order: 4th, M. Gilmartin, Sligo; 5th, M. Sweeney, Loughrea; 6th, R. O'Grady, Ballinrobe; 7th, P.J. Malone, Ballinrobe; 8th, B. Murphy, Ballinrobe; and 9th, Des Elliott, Dublin. The prize for the Heaviest Fish was won by Rev. Brother Denis Daly, Waterford, 2lbs 3ozs. Winning Boatmen in the Heats were: Jimmy Murphy, Tom Cusack and P. J. Malone. Best competing member of the Boatmens' Association and winner of the "Silver Perpetual Cup" presented by the late J. G. Wardrop went to Robbie O'Grady. Overseas prize winner was Fred Hartley and best North of Ireland prize winner was Tony O'Brien from Garrison, Co Fermanagh. Bart Crowley recalls motoring up the lake with his two competitors on one of the brighter and calmer mornings on that year smug in the knowledge that he did not have to fish, but was acting as boatman. As he was passing some submerged rocks he throttled back and commented to his two competitors about the clarity of the water. A Cork accent replied : "We have plenty clear water down in Cork boy" ; "It's a trout we want to see." 181 anglers participated in the competition but no further detail appears to be available.

## 1976 – Robbie O'Grady for 2nd time

The 12th annual trout angling wet fly fishing festival was announced by chairman Robbie O'Grady with a total of £700 in cash prizes commencing on 30th of July with three heats and the final on August 2nd. History was to be made this year because the World Cup winner of 1964 was to win again and become the first angler to win the World Cup Competition on two occasions. George Burrows reported in the Irish Times that every contestant at the Lough Mask 12th annual event was pleased at Robbie O'Grady's win with 7 trout, making 8lbs 11ozs in the final.

"Robbie has been long on the trail, helping the festival in all sorts of ways, as chairman, as boat manager, as general handyman, doing some unscheduled jobs that come to all organisers."

George Burrows continues : "He is an all-round sportsman, following the seasons with gun and rod – and dog. Indeed this country is lucky in having many like him – the impressive truth, which we should remember, is that we could never have too many of them."

Robbie O'Grady, 2nd time World Cup Winner, receives the Cup from John O'Flynn, Guinness Group Sales (Ireland).

**Extract from "Shooting a line with O'Grady" by Brian Clarke (1978)**

"With scarcely a verbal comma, he invites us to follow him up a queasy ladder propped against the wall, so that we can see his fly-tying bench in the loft. There are fly-dressing feathers everywhere. It looks like a chicken run the day after the fox got in. From amid the chaos, he hands me an exquisite Green Peter that he's just finished tying – then launches into five full minutes of mime and sound effects to describe a big fish he's lost on a similar fly not long before, on Lough Mask. It is, by all accounts, about par for the course in a first meeting with Robbie O'Grady of Ballinrobe. But O'Grady isn't just one of Irish angling's great characters: he's one of Ireland's great anglers, too. He's a dazzling exponent of the two traditional lough fishing styles – of the wet fly, in which a team of three or four flies is cast out ahead of the boat, and then retrieved near the surface; and a master, too, of the "dap" – the dappling on the surface of a natural insect from a line kept airborne by the breeze from the top of a very long rod."

At this stage Robbie was the only one to have won the World Cup twice which Brian Clarke described as the "Lonsdale Belt" in the highly specialised world of the traditional lough fisherman.

There was great excitement at Cushlough and in the town at having a 2 time winner of this great event. Robbie, who was Chairman of the Lough Mask Trout Festival Committee and whose boatman on this occasion was Jimmy Walsh, was presented with the Guinness Cut Glass Trophy, Ballinrobe Traders Perpetual Silver Cup and a cheque for £200 for the overall winner and also the Wardrop Cup for the best competing boatman by Mr John O'Flynn of Guinness Group Sales (Ireland) Ltd. In 2nd place was John Hearn, of Banbridge, Co Down with 3 fish weighing 6lbs 8ozs and 3rd was Dermot O'Hara, Sligo with 3 fish weighing 6lbs 2ozs. Mrs Kentgens from Oughterard won the prize for the best lady angler with 2 trout weighing 3lbs 5.5ozs. The Heaviest fish prize sponsored by Luke Higgins and the Bank of Ireland was won by Dermot O'Hara with a weight of 4lbs 6.5ozs. Overseas prize went to Ian Veenhuysen, Wieringen, Holland and The North of Ireland prize to Tony O'Brien, Garrison, Co Fermanagh. The team prize was won by Christy O'Loughlin and Denis Kelleher, Ballinrobe, Peter O'Malley, Kilconly and Barry Hind, England with 9lbs 14ozs. Best competing boatman was John Joe Malone, Ballinrobe. Finally, the Heat winners were as follows ; Friday, Denis Kelleher, Saturday, Vinnie O'Reilly, Headford and Sunday John Joe Malone, Ballinrobe. 196 anglers competed in that year and 356 trout were caught weighing 446 lbs in 294 rod days.

## 1977 – "Jaws" Film Star participates in Festival

The late Brendan O'Reilly, RTÉ Sportscaster and former Irish High Jump Champion opened the "Ballinrobe Trout Festival" on 23rd of July. The festival lasted for ten days and had a calender of events for each day. The Festival Chairman Eamonn Sreenan, a local Bank of Ireland staff member stated that the highlight would be the 4-day World Cup Competition. A sumptuous trout supper in the recently opened Curraghmore House with 200 tickets on offer would be another highlight. Famous Actor Robert Shaw who starred in the box office smash hit "Jaws" was to make a number of guest appearances during the Festival. Robert Shaw resided in Tourmakeady at the time. The whole idea of the festival was to generate more tourism interest in the area and the list of sporting activities was impressive by any standards. Included was a Regatta on the Robe and a canoe racing competition.

Carrol McHugh reported in the *Western Journal*: "Whether it was the fine weather or the revived interest in fishing, crowds flocked in their hundreds to the beautiful Cushlough Bay on the shores of Lough Mask for the World Cup Festival. A total number of 204 competitors fished in the four day competition. Many observers claimed that Lough Mask as a trout fishing lake was finished when pike were removed but that claim was discounted when 172 trout of over 200lbs weight were landed and those taking part would argue that the figures would be even higher if the weather (to the fishermen) was kinder."

After the qualifying rounds sixty anglers took to the boats to fish in the final. Mr Des Elliott, Dublin was successful with a catch of 3 fish weighing 3lbs 4ozs and won £200 and the Guinness Cut Glass Trophy. That was a very fine weekend on Lough Mask and as a result catches in the final heat and on Monday in the final were extremely poor. On Sunday's heat 76 rods only managed to weigh in 17 trout and in the final on Monday, a very fine bright day, rods weighed in 36 trout and the winning boatman was Tom Flanagan from Kilmaine. Second Prize winner was Peter O'Malley with 2 trout weighing 2lbs 12ozs, and in third place was none other than Tom Coucill, the original founding secretary of the event. Castlebar angler Larry Scott won the Heaviest Fish Prize with a trout weighing 2lbs 12ozs. A group of Dutch anglers which included Mr and Mrs Kentgens and Ed Van Wyk won the team prize and Mrs Kentgens was also the winning Lady Angler. Overseas Prize went to Ned Murphy and David Irvine, Lisburn was the winning North of Ireland entry. This year the team prize went to whom Competition Secretary, Tony Mulloy described as the Dutch Team, Mr and Mrs Kentgens, Ed Van Wijk and J. Van Wijk. Heat winners were as follows; Friday: J. Kentgens; Saturday: Peter O'Malley; Sunday: Louis Brennan, Tuam. The "Hat" was used to qualify a quota during the heats for this competition. This was a method devised to ensure that one in every three anglers competing would qualify for the final regardless of the catch. However, if one was fortunate to be drawn from the hat in order to make up the quota, the best one could hope for was 4th or following prizes. The reasoning behind this was that in order to qualify for 1st, 2nd or 3rd prize of the final day it was first necessary to catch fish in the qualifying heat. The heaviest fish prize was later added to this.

**Controversy over Curraghmore Housing Scheme – Fears over effects of Arterial Drainage**

Early in 1978 plans for the building of a housing scheme on the shores of Lough Mask met with objections by local fishermen who feared that fish life in the lake would be affected by sewage if houses were built there. Mayo Co Council granted planning permission to a Company to build a holiday village of 72 houses at Curraghmore, Ballinrobe, but an appeal against the granting of the permission had been made by Ballinrobe & District Trout Anglers' Association. The local Club were joined by An Taisce, Inland Fisheries'Trust, the Trout Angler's Federation of Ireland and the Connacht Angling Council in the appeal to the Planning Appeals Board, mainly on the grounds that the proposed sewage scheme as outlined in the plan was inadequate. The Official Launch of the "Robe

Catchment Drainage Scheme" which was to affect the whole Fishery took place at this time and a picket was manned in Main Street by the Ballinrobe Anglers Club objecting to the unacceptable lakeshore development, to coincide with the arrival of the Minister for the launch. Anglers from all over Ireland banded together as one with the local people and fought tooth and nail so that the water should remain as it always has been. The project was eventually over-ruled by An Bord Pleanála.

However the main River Robe drainage scheme got underway and soon the waters of Lough Mask, especially around the area from Cushlough to Lively Bay were to assume a brown murky colour as the drainage works progressed along the river. Earlier, a joint statement was issued by the ITFFA and TAFI with the backing of the Connaught Angling Council and all local Carra, Mask and Corrib Clubs outlining the threat to these fisheries posed by the forthcoming drainage scheme. Whilst realising that the farming community in the Upper Corrib/Mask catchment were entitled to the benefits of arterial drainage based on the premise that such schemes had already been carried out in other catchments, nevertheless a number of proposals were brought forward which would if implemented, act as safeguards for the future of the fishery.

Widespread unease was expressed among the angling fraternity at the impending arterial drainage scheme and its effects on the capacity of the River Robe as a main spawning area for supply of wild brown trout in numbers to the Lough Mask Fishery and following a meeting of all fishery interests a joint protest was sent to the Office of Public Works who were charged with implementing the drainage scheme.

Fears were expressed for the future of Lough Carra because of its shallow nature. The absolute necessity to maintain the weir on the Keel River, which connects Lough Carra with Mask, was emphasised. Lovers of Lough Carra, and there are many including myself can be thankful for the input of Ruaidhri De Barra and the Western Regional Fisheries Board at a later stage in negotiation in having some measure of success concerning the weir, thus saving Lough Carra as a fishery. But the River Robe was to suffer a severe setback as a major spawning river, and, although work is ongoing in the rehabilitation of this once great asset it has never recovered its former glory either as a fishing river in its own right or as a major spawning nursery for Lough Mask. Areas of the lake adjacent to the mouth of the Robe which gave excellent returns to the angler pre–drainage have never recovered their former glory. I think mainly of Lively Bay, Ramshorn and Golden Bays right down to the Rocky Shore on the north side of the lake, which had provided me with great sport over many years before the drainage scheme took place but has not returned fish in any great quantity since then.

# 1978 – Return of the World Cup

The hardworking Secretary of the World Cup competition Tony Mulloy told the *Western People* that agreed competition dates for 1978 were the 4th to the 7th August inclusive. Prize money was increased to £800 with numerous trophies including the original perpetual 1953 World Cup. During 1978 Atty McCormack, the hardworking Treasurer embarked on a mission to find out what became of the original 1953 World Cup. In April of that year following negotiations between Atty McCormack, Tony Mulloy, and Paddy Howard and Tom Coucill of the old Castlebar Angling Club the original cup was given to the existing committee who in turn agreed to make a donation to a nominated charitable organisation.

*Cecil Gibson, Crooked Wood, Mullingar, winner of the 1978 World Cup.*

The Cup had rested in the attic of a house in Castlebar and had sustained some superficial damages. Brian Geraghty of Bord Failte recalled visiting Atty McCormack around this time to see the Cup. Brian recalled that Atty told him that the Cup had some cement attached to it when returned. On asking Atty how he managed to separate the cement from the cup? "Vinegar" Atty replied. "Vinegar is a great cleaner you know, but I cannot be telling you all our secrets in Ballinrobe". The Cup had lain in an attic in Castlebar for 14 years and apart from the cement was in relatively good condition. Atty cleaned it until it was shining like new. The cup was then sent to Norman Pillow, a jeweller in Dublin with Ballinrobe connections, who carried out some necessary repairs and had all the winners names since it was last used in 1964 inscribed on the base. This added greatly to the competition and must be one of the most sought after Angling Cups in history today.

A further debate took place at this stage of development of the competition about the rights and wrongs of the "Hat". The debate was prompted by the fact that so many qualified to fish for the World Cup on the previous year "out of the hat" as already explained. Opinion among anglers was very divided on this issue and some people felt that anyone who qualified by being drawn from the hat should fish in a different competition with different prizes.

Meanwhile Mike Murphy of RTÉ fame performed the opening ceremony of the Ballinrobe Trout Festival which had a long list of events and included a spectacular boat show and fashion show. The Festival finished with a two day race meeting on August 21st and 22nd.

An entry fee of £15 was agreed on for the competition in 1978. An entry in the *Western People* in July to the effect that " last month at the River Plate Stadium in Buenos Aires, Argentina, through the hand of God and the head of Maradonna settled the argument as to who the best soccer players in the world were when they beat Holland in the World Cup Final." "Well in Ballinrobe next week-end there will also be a World Cup Final and this time to decide who the best fisherman in the World is".

Among the 224 reported competitors were anglers from 7 Countries and there were several changes to the prize schedule. First Prize was the World Cup, £200, the Guinness Cut Glass Trophy and Replica. Second Prize was a 4HP Outboard Motor sponsored by Burke Boats and third again sponsored by Burkes: A Silver Cup with £50 added. The return of the original World Cup was a big attraction.

In recent years the social side of the competition had been made more attractive and in 1977 many anglers brought their families to make it a holiday weekend. Guesthouses and hotels were full and the local serviced caravan park had its busiest weekend so far.

George Burrows reported in the *Irish Times* that all praise was due to Mr Cecil Gibson, so well known on Lough Derrevaragh, who won the World Cup with a catch of 3 trout weighing 4.99lbs. At the time in his 72nd year, a man of stamina and humour, an ardent angler and one of the best storytellers of angling yarns. A regular August Week-end visitor to Lough Mask from Crooked Wood, Mullingar, Mr Gibson, a well known farmer was also a well known G.A.A. follower and Referee. Mr Winston McConville, Tanderagee, Armagh the 1970 World Champion was 2nd with 4 fish weighing 4.46lbs and third was Brendan Foley of Balreask, Navan with 4 fish for 4.45lbs and the Lough Mask Boatmen's Assoc prize for 4th went to Con Hope, Mullingar with 3 fish for 4.28lbs.

George reported that Con Hope was a sort of ADC to Cecil Gibson during the flight west. George referred to the fact that the original World Cup was back in circulation and stated that if one is to judge by the Ballinrobe enthusiasm of that week-end it will be kept so – unless Lough Mask disappears as an angling lake.

68 anglers qualified for the final and they caught 60 fish weighing 88.72lbs. The leading lady angler was Mrs P. Donnelly, Dublin and the best overseas prize went to Mr M. McHugh of San Francisco.

Guest of Honour Mr Michael O'Malley, Co Manager in his address stated that everything possible must be done to safeguard our waterways from pollution. During the past year he was happy that Mayo Co Council in Co-operation with Bord Failte were able to build a Club House at Cushlough Bay. Mr O'Malley said that this was the beginning of many such developments.

224 anglers caught 172 trout in total weighing 232.81lbs in 292 angling days. George Burrows reported that it was not a great return, but fair enough when one takes into account the cold weather that was around at the time. Quite a number of fish were reported as having made good their escape after being hooked.

## 1979 – Another Day Added

In an article appearing in the *Trout Fisherman* of August 1979 Bob Church recalls a visit to Lough Mask when he stayed and fished with Robbie O'Grady. He recalls being regaled for a week with tales of flies, sure fire drifts and epic struggles with big fish. One of the encounters came when, as a teenager, Robbie was dapping with 3 Mayflies. He had the take at 8.30am and lost the massive trout, which leapt several heart-stopping times, a full mile away from where he had hooked it. Robbie estimated the trout at somewhere around the 17lb mark. Bob tried all kinds of lures without success on this occasion, apart from one small black Chenille lure fished on the top dropper. When Robbie peered in to the lure boxes, the look which came to his face was really something to see. He looked up at Bob and with a wry smile suggested that they would be better off kept in a cage and fed on meat!

An entry in the *Mayo News* in mid-July stated that 187 entries had been received and that there would be 4 Heats this year with the Thursday preceding the week-end becoming the extra Heat. The cash prize was increased to £240 for the winner.

Among the entries received was one from Malcolm Meintjes, Marshaltown, Transvaal, South Africa. I have a good memory of the final that year which was fished in near impossible conditions. We were all in the "Doldrums" on that day

*John Jennings, Rahard, Ballinrobe, 1979 World Cup Winner at Cushlough.*

as the lake was like a mirror with not as much as a ripple from Curraghmore to Tourmakeady. Boats commenced motoring for Cushlough Bay about 5.20 pm and we were one of the last boats to slowly and reluctantly leave the back of the Rialisk (Relligs) because it was obvious to us that one fish could in these conditions make a difference to the results. One boat persevered to the last minute however, and at the same time a ripple spread from the area near Devenish Island and quickly engulfed this area. Both anglers cast their flies into the ripple for a last chance. Up came a trout of 5.36 lbs weight and grabbed the "Green Peter" on local man John Jennings' cast and the next 10 minutes decided the destiny of the "World Cup".

John, a very popular local man was a staff member of the "North Western Regional Fisheries Board" at the time. The fish was played with due care before being netted. The engine was started and the boat roared for Cushlough Bay with all haste despite the rocks on either side in order to try and get inside the markers before the shotgun blast would bring matters to an end.

The *Western Journal* reports that Izaak Walton would have found the company genial in Ballinrobe as practitioners of the rod and line from many climes competed for the World Cup over August week-end. A new record of 268 anglers caught 282 trout weighing 376.41lbs in 334 rod-days giving an average weight of 1.33lbs

The weigh in was supervised by Garda Jim Moore and the prizes were presented at a dinner in the Valkenburg Hotel. Officers of the Committee on this occasion were Chairman: Denis Kelleher; Vice Chairman: Jimmy Murphy; Secretary: Tony Mulloy; Treasurer: Atty McCormack; Boat Manager: Robbie O'Grady; and PRO: John P. Burke.

John Jennings proved to be a very popular local winner with 2 trout weighing 6.79lbs and in 2nd place was Bill Colohan, Portumna with 3 fish weighing 5.67lbs. Bart Crowley from Kilrush, Co Clare but now living in Ballinrobe, took third prize with 2 fish weighing 4.34lbs. Miss Mary Rooney from Kinlough, Co. Leitrim who sat for her Leaving Certificate in June of that year was the only female devotee of the sport to qualify for the final and won the prize for the lady with the heaviest catch over the competition. The team prize that year was won by Rory's Fishing Tackle team captained by Rory Harkin of the famous Tackle Shop in Temple Bar, Dublin and a long time sponsor of the competition. The Ballinrobe Traders' Cup was presented to this team. Overseas prize was won by Joe Leonard of Southampton and North of Ireland prize to Tony O'Brien from Garrison, Co Fermanagh.

The World Cup Champion, John Jennings had the heaviest fish of the competition at 5.36lbs, but because he was overall winner that particular prize category went to the 2nd heaviest fish caught by Rory O'Moore, Cork with another fine trout of 5.33lbs. Finally the heat winners were as follows: Thursday, Bart Crowley, Ballinrobe with 3 fish weighing 5.65lbs, Friday; Denis Kelleher, Ballinrobe with 4 fish weighing 6.34lbs. Saturday: Bill Colohan Portumna, with 3 fish weighing 6.33lbs; and on Sunday Joe McBride, Dublin caught 6 fish weighing 7.32lbs to win that heat. Dermot O'Connor of the "Market House Tavern" sponsored and presented the Boatmens' prizes to the winner, Tom Cusack, 2nd Jackie Sullivan and 3rd Johnny Sheridan.

*Aerial view of Lough Mask from Gortmore area.*

# Chapter 4

## 1980 – "The Year of the Stockies"

The *Western People*, in a July report states that 2 Ballinrobe anglers who braved the inclement weather conditions on Lough Mask were fittingly rewarded. Tommy Walsh and Denis Kelleher landed 12 trout weighing 22lbs 12ozs, one of the best catches in recent years. However, much of the hype about this catch has to be discounted when one considers what was actually going on in the Lake at that time.

*Tommy Walsh collects his prize from Jimmy Murphy, Chairman.*

The Office of Public Works made some funding available to the Western Regional Fishery Board as a compensatory measure and for the first time Trout from the Fishery Board's Fish Farm in Roscrea were stocked into Lough Mask on a regular basis during this year.

*World Cup winner Louis Brennan, Tuam, is presented with Cup by Chairman D. Kelleher, 1980.*

My memory of the World Cup that year was of boats drifting, one after another in concentrated areas, but mainly well clear of the Cuslough to Lively Bay area as they pursued the now utterly confused new arrivals to Lough Mask with a fair degree of success as the competition results would show. The fish stands strained with fish each evening and many competitors who felt that they were safely qualified with their catches were in for a rude awakening following the weigh in each evening.

In the World Cup competition the same Tommy Walsh won the Saturday Heat with a catch of 8 trout weighing

9.25lbs and Kenneth, son of local angling specialist Robbie O'Grady qualified for the final at 14 years of age in the same Heat and went on to catch 4 trout weighing 4.27lbs in the final.

Tommy Walsh known affectionately among his friends as "Coffee" was one of the great characters on the local angling scene at the time and for many years afterwards. Tommy had a very short cast which was known to hit the water like a ton of bricks from time to time. The flies were retrieved immediately on the surface and allowed to float right up to the side of the boat before lift off at 100 mph and I am witness to the fact that he stirred as many fish as any angler and "captured" quite a few. Any new flies he purchased had to spend some time in Limbo where they underwent a fading process before being declared ready for use. The "Limbo" in question was the lapel of his jacket and while there the flies inherited a distinct tobacco flavour which may very well have added to their value when in use. I enjoyed many years of fishing with him and on our normally successful return journeys from Lough Inagh where we used to visit a few times each year in quest of the sea-trout and the occasional grilse, we would stop for some refreshments at a pub he called "Jam-Jars" an obvious reference to earlier times. Here after a few drinks the day's happenings were sometimes painfully recalled, "Stop. You struck too fast" and often he would explain why he never got married. "Stop, 'twas the high stool ruined me." Tommy was a great character and I have memories of great days on Carra as well as Mask with him.

Louis Brennan from Tuam fished the final that year with Paddy Maye as Boatman and had a very lively day at Caher Bay and the Curraghmore shore. Louis was particularly successful along this shore and the other competitor requested Paddy Maye to turn the boat around and give him a turn at the shore side where Louis was rising fish on the next drift. However, Paddy rightly was fearful for his engine which may come to grief on one of the rocks which they were brushing by. Louis agreed to change places with the other angler who had by now formed the distinct impression that the trout were being unfairly selective. No sooner had they commenced fishing once more in changed positions than Louis was into another fish. They met fish for most of the day and in the evening Louis had a catch of 7 trout weighing 8.29lbs which was good enough to win the day.

In 2nd place was George Burrows, Malahide, Dublin, the well known *Irish Times* angling correspondent, journalist and broadcaster with 7 trout weighing 8.13lbs and third was Fergus Dornan, Lisburn, with a catch of 6 trout weighing 7.61lbs. Winner of the Heaviest Fish Prize that year was Cyril O'Donnell from Cork and for the first time there was no local name in the first 7 catches. To give an idea of how closely placed the catches were, only 3.21 lbs separated 1st and

10th prize weight which was 5.08lbs. Local angler Dr. Christy Guckian came 8th with a catch of 5 fish for 5.35lbs. I remember his reply when I congratulated him because I thought that it was unusual. " I'm happy because I beat the other Doctors". One would be forgiven for assuming that high on the list of necessary criteria to get a medical practitioner appointment in Ballinrobe at the time was a good understanding of the art of Fly Fishing for trout. All three Doctors are now no longer with us and both Dr Cummins and Dr McDarby were also keen anglers.

There were 67 finalists of which 51 anglers caught 168 trout weighing 185.5lbs. In what was a record catch, even if they were "Stockies" 271 anglers caught 984 trout weighing 1078.75lbs. Other results of the competition were as follows: Overseas prize to J. Leonard, Southampton; Ladies Prize to Mrs Kentgens, Oughterard; North of Ireland Prize to Sam. J. Proctor, Co. Down. Team prize to M. Brennan, J. Ireland, S. Downey and T. Boyd of Lisburn. Winning Boatman: Paddy Maye, 2nd, Johnny Sheridan and 3rd, Seán Smith.

## 1981 – A Winner from Derry

Karl J. Henry, a bank official from Draperstown, Co Derry, Northern Ireland became the 1981 World Cup Champion with PJ Malone as Boatman and in 2nd

*Karl Henry, 1981 winner, received cup from Jimmy Murphy, Chairman.*

place was Joe Leonard of Southampton with 6 fish weighing 6.48lbs. 3rd from Belfast with 2 fish weighing 4.40lbs was J. Brennan. Des McHugh, USA was 5th with 4 fish for 4.19lbs. The Luke Higgins Cup for the Heaviest Fish was won by John Lewin, Drogheda with a trout weighing 2.75lbs and the Team Prize went to R. O'Grady, Billy Murphy, John Lewin and Brendan Costello. 71 anglers caught 48 fish weighing 49.61lbs on Thursday's heat and heat winner was Joe Leonard, a Cong born Dentist based in Southampton whose catch was 4 fish weighing 4.83lbs followed by Ed Van Wijk, Holland with 2 fish for 2.18lbs and Frank Smyth, Drogheda, a former winner with 1 fish for 2.15lbs. W. K. Brayden with a catch of 4 trout weighing 4.15lbs won Friday's heat that year with boatman Eamon Sheridan. Saturday's and Sunday's heats were won by Des McHugh, USA and E. Armstrong, Sligo respectively. The boatman who brought in the winner that year was P.J. Malone, and other boatmen to win prizes were Tom Cameron, Johnny Sheridan and Eamon Sheridan. 68 competitors qualified for the final, of which 43 weighed in 99 fish totalling 99.02lbs. 276 anglers caught 373 trout weighing 392 lbs.

The Ballinrobe news in the *Western People* of 7th August records that Mr Tony Mulloy, retired headmaster of Ballinrobe Vocational School, was the recipient of a presentation of Waterford Glass from the Neale Dramatic Society. Prior to this Tony had given long and distinguished service to the World Cup Committee and had performed the important duties of a Secretary with distinction for the previous fifteen years, the longest period of service on record in the past 50 years. Athough not an angler himself he has many angling friends whom he met over the years. Tony and Bridie Mulloy ran a guesthouse in Main Street, Ballinrobe which was a favourite base for anglers at this time and with Tony as Secretary and Atty McCormack as Treasurer the World Cup Competition was in safe hands. Both Tony and Bridie maintain a great interest in the competition to the present time.

## 1982 – Another Winner from Louth

The *Western People* reported that over £4,000 worth of prizes would be available to competitors and 50 places would be reserved for overseas anglers. The angler who is lucky enough to bring in the winning catch in the final would receive prizes to the value of £1,600 for the first time. Big news on the sponsorship front was that the World Cup Committee had for the first time secured sponsorship of a 19' Lake Angling Boat through the good offices of the Secretary John P. Burke of Burke Boats and Western Fibreglass Mouldings. John P. Burke was competition Secretary and founder member Jimmy Murphy was Chairman with Denis Kelleher as PRO and Michael Harness as Boat Manager. Michael became proprietor of the "Anchor Bar" in Bridge St, Ballinrobe and many anglers were attracted to this new pub which became like a shrine to the World Cup, with photograpgs of the annual winners adorning the main wall.

George Burrows reported that the Lough Mask trout went on extended holiday covering the August Bank Holiday, when the final of the World Cup contest was fought against a lot of odds. The four days of heats were well named, for the sun never faltered between 11am and 6pm. except on the Saturday when the sky over Tourmakeady opened briefly with a deluge which soaked all, and for a shower on Sunday. On Final day the catch was not too impressive due to fine conditions. Jim Stafford, a native of Drogheda had arrived in Ballinrobe and worked as a Staff member of the Inland Fisheries Trust and was then with the Central Fisheries Board and despite the fine conditions had managed to catch 3 trout weighing 3lbs 7ozs with Tom Lynagh as boatman. This was good enough to make him World Cup Champion for 1982. In 2nd place came Mike Sweeney, Loughrea and Dublin who had already won the Lough Conn contest that year. Mike had 2 fish for 2lbs 5ozs and 3rd was John Stone of Nenagh with 2 fish weighing 1lb 13.5ozs. Winston McConville's team from the North of Ireland won the team prize that year and Miss Muriel Wilson, Dublin, won the Ladies Prize in addition to a heat prize.

*1982 Winner, Jim Stafford, receives World Cup from Jimmy Murphy, Chairman.*

Fred Hartley, St Helens, Lancashire, won the overseas prize and Jack Spratt, Antrim won the Northern Ireland prize. Heaviest fish Prize was won by W.J. Browne, Armagh at 2lbs 4.5ozs. The Boatman who brought in the winner that year was Tom Lynagh. 86 anglers contested the final and 24 caught 30 fish with a total weight of 33lbs 7ozs in poor conditions. Conor Maguire, Dublin with 4lbs 1.5ozs won Thursday's heat and on Friday it was the turn of Peter O'Malley, Cloghans Hill, Tuam with 3 fish weighing 3lbs 8 ozs. Michael Sweeney, Loughrea, was victorious on Saturday with 2 fish weighing 3lbs 10ozs and Miss M. Wilson, Dublin with 2 fish weighing 2lbs 10 ozs. was the final heat winner on Sunday. P.J. Malone and Sean Walsh were also prize winning boatmen in this competition. A total of 348 anglers caught 184 trout weighing 181lbs in 434 rod-days.

George Burrows reported that the social side was lively with a hectic incident at the dinner, caused by a gentleman who, having reached his quota at the bar earlier on, kept "rising" like an eager trout, yet always coming short, in angling terms. But all was settled joyfully. Micheál Breathnach, the Secretary of the Central Fisheries Board spoke with steady enthusiasm regarding Ireland's angling, yet apologised for lack of money for development because of Finance Minister McSharry's budget.

In competitions of this size, the role played by the boatman is crucial, and more often than not, anglers would be well advised to leave the selection of the fishing ground to him. As a safety measure, he has the final say in the destination but more often than not will consult with the anglers and arrive at a consensus. There is the story of an irate boatman on Lough Conn some years ago when confronted with two very different location requests for the days fishing suggested that he would go ashore and get the chainsaw if he heard anymore. In that way he could make two boats out of one and each angler could float off to his preferred destination!

## 1983 – Sligo Angler Wins World Cup

John P. Burke, Secretary to the World Cup sponsored a Burke "Anglers' Fancy Fibre Glass Boat" as part of 1st prize for the 2nd year and this added greatly to the value of the 1st Prize. Morans' Sawmills and the "Lakeland Hotel"

*Brendan Smith, 1983 winner, with runners-up, Jimmy McDonald and Peter O'Reilly C.F.B., Cavan.*

sponsored £200 towards 1st prize and this was added to the Guinness Waterford Glass Trophy and the World Cup. 298 competitors took part that year and the competition was reckoned to be worth £25,000 to the immediate local economy. Visitors from the USA, France, Germany, The Netherlands, the UK and a large entry from the North of Ireland were reported to have taken part.

*Mr. and Mrs. Brendan Smith with the winning catch 1983.*

Jimmy Murphy, Chairman of the organising committee introduced the guest of honour Mr Paddy O'Toole, Minister for Fisheries at the final presentation and dinner. The Minister, in a wide ranging address referred to the value of trout angling alone to tourism at that time as £7 million per annum. He spoke of the rehabilitation programme for the Fishery which was underway at that time following the Arterial Drainage Scheme carried out by the Office of Public Works in recent times.

The Competition took place from the 28th July to the 1st of August that year and once more a portion of the overall catch was made up of the "stockies" which were introduced to Lough Mask during the Robe Drainage.

The World Cup winner was Brendan Smith from Sligo a popular and regular Lough Mask angler who had a fantastic competition that year. Brendan also won his qualifying Heat on the Friday with 6 trout weighing 5.53 lbs with local man Paddy Maye as Boatman. His winning catch on the final day was also 6 trout weighing 7.49lbs and his winning Boatman was P. Horan, Partry In 2nd place was Jimmy McDonald, Ballinrobe, with a catch of 3 trout weighing 4.96lbs and third prize winner was well known Central Fisheries Board Staff Member, Peter O'Reilly with 3 trout weighing 3.65lbs.

The Heaviest Fish Winner was G. A. Cawley, Crossmolina with 4.56lbs and other Heat Winners were as follows: Saturday – R. T. Marshall, Newtownabbey, Co Antrim with 7 fish weighing 6.59lbs. On Sunday – Cyril Murray, Galway with 4 trout weighing 5.81lbs and on Thursday – Frank Smith, Drogheda, with 5 trout weighing 5.94lbs. A total number of 298 anglers participated and caught 394 trout weighing 477lbs 12ozs.

# 1984 – World Cup for Germany

Ballinrobe and District Trout Anglers convened a meeting of several local clubs to discuss the planned operations of the Office of Public Works at the Canal. The intention of the OPW was to deepen the Lough Mask/Corrib canal by blasting the rock bed, the object being to increase the outflow of water from Lough Mask during times of sustained rainfall. The canal was originally cut through limestone with the intention of providing a navigable waterway between the two lakes, which would have commercial possibilities at the time. Some of the infrastructure to facilitate this development was put in place on the Robe River at Ballinrobe where bollards to assist in mooring boats can still be seen. The Salmon Weir Bridge on the Bowers' Walk still exists although there is no evidence that a salmon ever came near it because, as we now know the whole project collapsed when the water disappeared down through the porous limestone. As a result of the meeting a letter was drafted and sent to the various authorities outlining in detail, the fears of the local community and requesting that the blasting be stopped and other measures be used to undertake this work.

*Kurt Menrad*

The town of Ballinrobe came to a grief-stricken halt on Friday 6th of July as town people, neighbours and others from a wide surrounding area joined in the mourning for a father and his two children lost in a Lough Mask boating tragedy which was the worst recorded in recent times. On the previous Sunday pm / Monday am, a night and early morning of unbelievable tragedy and great personal courage, three members of a family died and two others and a cousin were saved. All local boatmen and anglers were on the lake from dawn until dusk on Monday 2nd when the search resulting from this extremely sad tragedy was brought to a conclusion.

In early August one of the best and most international results the World Cup Committee could hope for happened in the 1984 competition when a German, Kurt Menrad won the competition with a catch of 2 trout for 3.89lbs and in 2nd place came the very well known English angler, Bob Church with 3 trout weighing 3.75lbs. Third place went to local angler John Nestor, who was a member of the organising committee with 2 trout weighing 3.58lbs. All three men were extremely well known and very popular winners. Kurt Menrad, who was presented with the World Cup by Committee Chairman, Michael Harnesse, came to Ireland some years earlier and set up Caidéil MP Teoranta in Tourmakeady. This provided some badly needed employment in that area with the manufacture of atomizers as used with perfume and other products. Caidéil is still with us today and unlike many of our industrial development stories of those times, is trading as a highly successful Company. One of Kurt's early battles was to have facilities for a fax/telex machine installed and improved telephone services to enable him continue in business from the Caidéil factory in Tourmakeady. Thankfully we have moved on from those days. Kurt fell in love with Lough Mask at an early stage and set up home in Tourmakeady where he graduated from trolling to fly fishing at an early stage. He was very generous with sponsorship for both the World Cup Competition and a similar competition which was fished from Gortmore Bay and always had fishery development and conservation matters close to his heart. Installed in his boat was a fish tank and whenever he caught a trout over the 12 inch limit, the fish was placed carefully in the tank for safe keeping, later to be returned, should Kurt be lucky enough to catch a larger one. This was at a time when most anglers were taking every fish they caught over the limit. Thankfully the attitude of most anglers today has changed dramatically and nowadays, if an angler berths at Cushlough or any other landing area around the lake after a day's fishing with a large catch of trout, far from being marvelled at he will be frowned upon by his peers.

It is true to say that Kurt Menrad played his part in bringing about this change in mindset by suggesting that the larger competitions like the World Cup should also become more conscious of sustainable development and conservation by making funding available from the proceeds of competitions towards this end. Valuable extra sponsorship was obtained from Kevin Duffy in partnership with the Main Johnson Importer who presented a 9.9 HP Johnson Outboard Engine which would join the 18ft 10inches Anglers' Fancy Fibreglass Boat already sponsored by John P Burke of Burke Boats, Secretary of the Competition, and add greatly to the value of the 1st Prize in 1984 and following years. Entry Fee was held at £35.

340 competitors took part from Northern Ireland, England, France, Germany, and the USA. The weather conditions were moderately good to fine and a very large crowd attended the weigh in each evening. Fifty-four anglers competed in the first Heat on Thursday August 2nd and the first 14 qualified for the final. M. Brennan, Belfast, won the heat. 19 of the 73 anglers qualified from the 2nd Heat and the winner was N. Reddy from Sligo. Ivan Sproule won Saturday's heat and John Jennings caught a 4.68 lb trout to record the Heaviest fish of the competition. Miss Elizabeth Black, Northern Ireland, had a fish also to win the Ladies prize with 2.23lbs. Kevin Duffy of Headford who had 3 fish weighing 4.58lbs won Sunday's heat. In all 223 fish were caught over the 5 days. The total weight was 251.87lbs and for the first time in Irish angling history the results were computerised and the Committee thanked Mr Art O'Sullivan of "Micro Education West" who operated the computer and programme.

# 1985 – Back to Westport Again

The 1985 brochure for the World Cup launched by Chairman Matt Moran proudly proclaimed that the value of 1st prize had now risen to £2,500 and included the Guinness sponsored Waterford Cut Glass Trophy, an Anglers Fancy 18' 10" Fibre Glass Boat sponsored by Burke Boats and a 9.9 HP Johnson Outboard Engine sponsored by Kevin Duffy & Sons, Headford. With 4 Heats and a final the competition accommodated 371 anglers and among them were Peter Thomas, a former Captain of the English International Team and the well known English Angler from Northampton Bob Church.

Dark overcast skies, heavy rain and strong gales brought trout up in the big waves for which Mask is noted. While it was not the type of weather the tourist industry hopes for, if one could brave the big waves it was ideal enough for the Wet Fly Angler. Each boat carries two anglers decided by draw but every attempt is made for visiting anglers, new to the lake, to fish beside locals. Boatmen are always drawn also and a set of rules has evolved over the years to cover most eventualities. A number of years ago the overall winner ceased fishing on the final day with 2 hours of the competition left. He got frightened at the size of the waves and asked to be put ashore in Tourmakeady, about 12 miles by land from the starting point. He was amazed to discover that he was later declared the winner. However, the rules were changed to cover this eventuality and now every angler is obliged to hand in his own catch.

Peter Thomas gives a particularly good description of his experience that year. "It's a thrilling sight, once the starting signal has been given to watch the boats manoeuvre from the stages, then tug their engines into life, as they thread with caution down the narrow channel that leaves the bay, before finally opening the throttle. Now the whole armada splits, furrowing the Lough with long trails of foam as each heads in hope for the chosen ground – a kind of water-borne version of a Red Arrows display."

Bob Church recalls getting some rather Irish advice from Robbie O'Grady: "The secret is not to let the fish take you." "Rather you must take the fish" before he set out from Cushlough Bay on the morning of his heat. His boat partner was John Maye, himself an experienced boatman and angler, while the fresh-faced young boatman Ronan Cusack announced that he had brought in heat winners on Friday and Saturday and it was true with local men John Joe Malone and Denis Kelleher winning both heats with Ronan on the same year. Both anglers must have felt that they would certainly be covering trout on the day with Ronan, however maybe they also felt somewhat intimidated, and that anything short of a third Heat win would not satisfy the young Boatman. As it happened the law of averages was to reassert itself. They motored carefully down the lake into the increasing wind that pushed white spray into their faces and hair. Other boats were bouncing out of the water as they crashed into the full fury of the waves. Bob found himself mentally checking his buoyancy aid, or working out how far it would be to swim to the nearest island. Ronan spotted the rocks however, and they settled for drifting the more sheltered water around Inishmaine Island. Fish were hard to come by with a few rises coming out of the blue when they drifted over shallow water near the rocks. Further out in the lake, the wind was now so strong that it was almost impossible to remain in contact with the flies.

During the continual downpour that marred that day the wind actually eased but soon started to swing around and blow from the other end of the lake. Now, instead of motoring home with the wind they contested the waves once again. Both Bob and John lost good fish at the end of the day as they headed back for Cushlough where they failed to qualify on this occasion.

Bob also recalled the difficulty of trying to squeeze into Art O'Neill's Bar at 11pm. " A heady mixture of tobacco smoke and Guinness does nothing for the fishing to follow." "If you can twang a guitar or banjo, then rest assured that you

*Matt Moran, Chairman, presents the World Cup to Joe Berry, Westport, 1985 winner. Included in the photograph are Jimmy Burke (Sponsor), Mrs. Teresa Berry, Kevin Duffy (Sponsor), and Johnson Agent.*

will be joining one of the impromptu sing alongs that keep the town swinging until the early hours." [sic]

Talk of the fishing, however, is never far away. The day's results are posted up in every sponsoring Bar in town and Green Peters, Murroughs and Mayflies can be purchased as you enjoy a drink, with a great selection available at the Biggins "Corner House" Bar which in latter years has been invaded with anglers. In 1985 Art O'Neill would give you odds on winning if you were a betting man. Art O'Neills Bar was formerly the Luke Higgins owned "Eagle House", one of the best known angling Pubs in the West of Ireland from early World Cup years.

The four heats were fought out in wet windy conditions as already mentioned. Peter O'Malley, a local Irish International angler won Thursday's heat with 2 trout weighing 4.80lbs and with Richard Cameron as Boatman. Local well known boatman and angler, arguably one of the best, John Joe Malone won Friday's heat with 3 trout weighing 4.47lbs with Ronan Cusack boating. Denis Kelleher won Saturday's heat with 2 fish weighing 4.07lbs but all were well outdone on Sunday when Mike Sweeney from Loughrea weighed in 5 trout weighing 11.05 lbs with Ronan's father, Joe Cusack as boatman.

On the final day another very well known angler, angling administrator, Fly Tier and Boatman, Vinnie O'Reilly was drawn with Joe Berry of Westport and they chose to visit Stantons' Bay where Joe rose 17 trout in sheltered shallow water hooking 7. However the new size limit of 12 inches indicated that all fish were marginally under the limit. All competitors noted that many small fish were rising during that competition.

Joe Berry's luck changed however when two fish well over the limit came to his bobbing Golden Olive Bumble and a third and bigger fish later grabbed his "Bibio" on the tail. Joe succeeded in catching all three, and much to his amazement after seeing Mike Sweeney's magnificent catch on the previous day, Joe became a very popular winner of the World Cup with 3 fish weighing 3.94lbs. In 2nd place was J. Campbell also of Westport with 2 fish weighing 3.91lbs and 3rd was Christy Molamphy from Clonlara, Co Clare with 2 fish weighing 3.17lbs. Winner of the overseas prize (The Cushlough House Perpetual Cup with £20 added and a week-end for two at Cushlough House) for Northern Ireland or overseas angler with best catch over the competition was Peter Thomas with a trout of 3.90lbs. Peter also won the Luke Higgins Perpetual Challenge Cup, £55 sponsored by the Bank of Ireland and a free entry to the 1996 World Cup for the Heaviest Fish. The Ladies prize was won by Ms Elizabeth Black, Northern Ireland. Bank of Ireland sponsored Team prize winners were : Peter O'Malley, Denis Kelleher, T. Horler and Al McDonnell and best Ballinrobe Angler prize was won by Peter

*Chairman Matt Moran presents a prize to Vinnie O'Reilly, Headford.*

O'Malley. Overall statistics for the competition were as follows : In 464 rod days 170 of a total of 371 anglers caught 260 trout weighing 349.90 lbs, or an average weight of 1.35lbs.

Having competed in the competition, qualified and fished the final in 1985 as he had done for many a year before this, Richard O'Mahony of Main St, Castlelyons, Co Cork fell ill and died at Dermot O'Connors premises in Ballinrobe following the final of the competition. We remember Richard as a keen angler and a great supporter of the competition.

## 1986 – World Cup For Fermanagh

The 1986 World Cup competition took place from the 31st July to the 4th of August with J. J. Duffy as Chairman of the World Trout Fly Committee for that year. The winner and 1986 World Champion was Brian Hallet, Beleek, Co. Fermanagh with 2 trout weighing 3.41lbs and in 2nd place was W. McCartney with 2 trout weighing 2.64lbs and 3rd was UK angler Peter Thomas, a former English international team captain with 1 fish weighing 2.47lbs. 4th was Robbie O'Grady, Ballinrobe with 2 fish for 2.07lbs. 21 anglers caught 24 trout in the final weighing 29.12lbs and this suited the prize schedule for that year admirably because there were exactly 21 prizes on the final day.

Every type of weather that goes to make an Irish Summer or indeed, Winter was experienced on the lake with high winds on Thursday and Friday changing to heavy showers and moderate winds on Saturday. Some sunshine prevailed on Sunday and Monday but it was accompanied by thundery showers and almost flat calm conditions.

The Thursday Heat was won by Frank Hession, Tuam with 4 trout weighing 5.47lbs. On Friday Leo Joyce, the 1956 World Champion from Westport won the heat with 2 trout weighing 4.88lbs. On Saturday UK International angler Peter Thomas won the Heat with 4 fish weighing 5.48lbs, which was the best individual catch over the competition and on Sunday W. McCartney won with 1 fish weighing 3.77lbs. P.J. McNulty was the Heaviest Fish Winner with a trout of 4.07lbs. 394 anglers caught 220 fish weighing 296.78lbs in 496 rod days over the competition.

It is interesting to note that that many of the non qualifiers fished nearby Lough Carra and in the ten days leading to the end of the World Cup returns show that 480 trout weighing 690lbs were taken. These returns included a 6lbs, two 5lbs and several over 3lbs. Also on Carra, Watson Mills and Bru Meehan, regular anglers to the World Cup competition from Mullingar reported 46 fish for 5 days. On the final evening local Boatman Patsy Bradley was approached by another Boatman who jibed : "Well you didn't bring in the winner Patsy"! – To whom Patsy responded without blinking an eye " Upon my oath it would be hard for me when I didn't bring him out"!

*John J. Duffy, Chairman, presents the 1986 Cup to Brian Hallett, Beleek, Co. Fermanagh.*

## 1987 – Kells, County Meath and World Cup Champions

The 1987 competition was fished in relatively good conditions and attracted an all-time record entry of 427 anglers who caught 371 fish weighing 449.28lbs in 536 rod-days. The winner on this occasion was Hughie McLoughlin of Kells, Co Meath with a catch of 4 trout weighing 5lbs 11.5ozs. Hughie was to be the first of a number of successful competitors from that part of the country. The people of Kells gave Hughie a great welcome home and his victory was celebrated in style and rivalled the welcome accorded the Wesport winners in the 1950s. Second place went to Sean O'Loughlin, Ulster Bank, Wexford, with 2 fish weighing 3lbs 13.25ozs and 3rd was Denis Kelleher with 1 fish weighing 3lbs 11.75ozs.

I have pleasant memories of that weekend while fishing near Inisgleasty. The first day nearly ended in disaster for me when a misdirected cast made in squally weather during Friday's heat had the affect of driving one of the flies into my thumb. My Boatman Johnny Hopkins reacted admirably however, and had us on the Island within seconds. I would be obliged to give him full marks also for his surgical skills, as I was debating calling it a day and going for medical attention. At any rate Johnny released the Green Peter with the minimum of fuss and when we had our lunch and repaired casts we resumed once more our quest for qualification.

*Hughie McLoughlin, Kells, Co. Meath (centre), World Cup Winner 1987, pictured with winning Boatman, Tom Cameron. John Jennings, 1979 winner, is on the right.*

*Captain T. S. Joyce, Irish Ferries, makes a presentation to Phil Brookes, Best Overseas Competitor.*

As we rowed away from Inisgleasty in relatively calm conditions another competitors' boat came quite close to us and turned in the gap towards Dringeen leaving the usual disturbance of a seagull engine in its wake. I still remember throwing a cast right in where the boat had gone in very shallow boulder strewn water. As I retrieved the rod tightened and I was certain I had snagged a rock. However, the rock began to move! After a tremendous tussle in the deeper water I succeeded in taking a 4.55lb trout to a size 12 Bibio on the point and my day was completely transformed. However, the rule book prevailed against me on this occasion and I could not claim the prize for the heaviest fish because of getting third place on the final day. Other Heat winners that year were: Thursday – Frank Garvey, Corofin, Co Clare, 3 fish – 4.96lbs; Friday – Denis Kelleher, Ballinrobe – 4.55lbs; Saturday – Peter Thomas, Rutland, UK – 2 fish – 6.57lbs; and Sunday – P Toner, Sligo, 2 fish – 5.29lbs. The UK team of Peter Thomas, R. Holgate, J. Baldock and Phil Brooks won the team prize for the best catch.

Shortly after the competition storm clouds of dissent grew more menacing as the Government of the day brought forward proposals for the introduction of a rod licence for trout fishing. This was to have a catastrophic effect on the whole angling scene resulting in the cancellation of the World Cup and other Competitions for the following three years. For the first time in many years Cushlough Bay and many other Bays were silent places for August week-end.

The death of another of our Committee members, namely Paddy Varley, who helped for many years with this competition is recorded with regret at this time also.

**The Rod Licence Dispute**

Much has been written about the events that took place for the next two and a half years and probably the saddest happening was to see lifelong angling friends falling out with one another in different parts of the country but especially here in the West. I have no wish to add anything to what has been said already at a time when the worst effects of the dispute are receding into the distance other than to say that from the moment action was taken against elderly anglers who had their fishing equipment confiscated on the Corrib at an early stage in this dispute when they fished without a licence the dye was cast.

The perceived threat of fish rearing cages being installed at Lough Na Fooey and other areas to facilitate the rearing of Parr by private concerns for salmon farming to the detriment of wild fish stocks if the Government took complete control was not vehemently denied as scaremongering. The single most important factor was the inability of TDs in Senior Cabinet Posts particularly in the West to read the situation correctly as outlined by their constituents on many occasions and at many meetings. This insured that the row would run its course over an extended period of time. If this problem arose in the Fifties I feel that Micheál Ó Móráin, the former Minister already referred to in this book, would have handled the matter differently.

*"Now the whole armada splits furrowing the lough with long trails of foam"*
*– Peter Thomas.*

# Chapter 5

## 1991 – World Cup Resumes

Officers for the 1991 competition were President Atty Mc Cormack, Chairman and PRO, Denis Kelleher, Hon Secretary, Ray Owens, Boat Manager, Michael Harnesse and Treasurer John Nestor. Committee members were Joe Cusack, Robbie O'Grady, Bart Crowley, Jimmy Murphy and Michael McDarby.

The *Western People* reported that Ballinrobe boomed at the week-end when the World Cup Trout Fly was re-staged after an absence of three years. An estimated spin-off of £100,000 for the local economy put the smiles back on the faces of hard-pressed business people, who had experienced the wettest and worst early Summer of almost a decade and other areas of the county had not fared well with tourism numbers dwindling.

Belgian angling magazine publisher Guito Vitz, who is also one of the World's most celebrated competition flycasters was reported to be "delighted" with the way the Mask fished.

Caidéil MP Teoranta and the ESB joined our main sponsors on this occasion. Caidéil were jointly sponsoring the 1st prize with Burke Boats and the ESB looking after 2nd Prize together with Kevin Duffy of Headford. Irish Ferries with valuable prizes for overseas competitors and Brother International Ltd were also regular sponsors at this stage as were Warnants and a host of local sponsors. Robbie O'Grady got together with his Suppliers and sponsored a mountain bike. The annual input of Harry Smith of SKS Communications, both in supply of material and time insured that the Competition had a highly professional siren start and finish in addition to a quality P.A. system. Harry continues to

*Chairman, Denis Kelleher presents the 1991 World Cup to winner Brendan Moran, Kells, Co. Meath.*

supply this service to the present time.

The most important point about all this sponsorship was that we were enabled as a committee to make a grant towards Fishery Development in the area. The major objective of the competition since its inauguration was the further development of tourism and that had not changed over the years.

Statistics for the competition were as follows: 418 anglers competed, slightly under the number who fished in 1987, and in 524 rod days caught 231 trout weighing 325.25lbs. The World Cup returned to Kells for a 2nd year and the winner on this occasion was Brendan Moran with a catch of 1 trout weighing 3.95lbs. Only 16 fish were weighed in for the final which was a very bright sunny day and not really suitable for the sport. Joe Crean from Roundstone came 2nd with 2 fish weighing 3.47lbs and third was Bill Heritage of Warnants Exp Imp Co., one of our sponsors of long standing, with a catch of 2 trout weighing 2.30lbs. The winning boatman was Brian Joyce of Derrypark. Heat winner on Thursday was local man Martin Groonell with 1 trout weighing 2.84lbs. Padraig Munroe, Partry, won the Friday heat with 3 trout for 5.49lbs and M Kearney, Dublin won on Sunday with 3trout weighing 7.79lbs. On Sunday David Greham from Co Armagh won the final heat with 2 fish weighing 6.38lbs and this included a trout of 5.56lbs. Average weight of trout caught was 1.41lbs.

## 1992 – A year of major growth

The founding fathers of the World Cup in 1953 would never have envisaged that the competition would reach the stage where five or six hundred anglers would participate in the event and there is no doubt that the excellent boat management exercised over a period of years was a major factor in the growth of these numbers. Another factor undoubtedly was the growing number of competitors who agreed to give their services as boatmen for the duration of the event. The number of "regular" or "professional" boatmen available was on the decline for a number of years at this stage and at Mayfly time many visiting anglers were arriving with their own boats and engines. Most of these would have been introduced to the lake by local boatmen and would have built up some knowledge of what lay before them before venturing forth on their own The ability of one Michael Harnesse as boat manager to harness (pardon the pun) these anglers as a positive force to act as boatmen for the World Cup competition at this time was a considerable factor in the growth of the competition.

The 1992 competition marked the beginning of a period of unprecedented growth and also recorded the greatest increase of numbers competing in any one year. 545 anglers caught 302 fish weighing 406.3lbs. in 682 rod days.

There are many stories about this particular competition. The experience of the late Matthew Kennedy from Nenagh who did not enjoy the best of health at this time was recalled by Phil Brookes.

"Mattie in his heat, brought in the largest trout of this competition, a leviathan 6lbs 15ozs and had this fish and another 2 pound trout in the boat at 12 noon, or one hour after the start of the heat, so he had a fairly relaxed day after that and cruised home in the evening to win his heat. His partner, Vinnie O'Reilly from Headford also qualified easily with the result that a good day was had by both anglers with P. J. Feerick as boatman."

Matthew Kennedy knew at this stage that he had a great chance of winning the "Heaviest Fish" prize, but in order to qualify for this prize he could not finish in the first three places of the Final Day. He went out on final day, having drawn the same boatman again and succeeded in coming in fourth place on final day, thus maximising his winnings.

Phil Brookes was introduced to the area through participation in the competition and is now a regular visitor to Ballinrobe and makes the point that the competition is emphatically not about winning; it is about taking part which is everything. Undoubtedly, it is everyone's dream to get through to the final. However, failure or success at any stage is celebrated equally, long and hard, in the many friendly and sympathetic bars in Ballinrobe. Phil has become a close ally of the committee and has been described as our World Cup ambassador in the UK.

Another story which survives since 1992 is that of the experience of Johnny Ray from Belcoo, Co Fermanagh. Phil relates that while Johnny was fishing the Thursday heat under the stewartship of well known local ghillie and two-time World Cup winner Robbie O'Grady, he hooked a very big trout, reckoned to be a gillaroo of 7 or 8 pounds. The fish was brought close to the net twice, but in typical gillaroo fashion made one last dash for freedom and got itself wedged under a rock. In one last effort Johnny stripped down to his bare essentials and went in after the fish. He actually went under three times, net in hand before giving up. I hasten to add that neither the committee or the boatmen would recommend a repeat of this performance.

My best memory of this competition is on final day when I was lucky enough to be drawn with the eventual winner but almost got a chance to overtake him with his own fly. Sean Maguire from Garrison, Co Fermanagh a member of a very sporting family well known North and South was my partner and agreed with an early decision to cross the lake to the Tourmakeady shore and commence

*Kurt Menrad, Sponsor (World Cup Winner 1984); Martin Murphy (Sponsor); Seán McGuire, Garrison, Co. Fermanagh, Winner 1992; Denis Kelleher; Dermot Treacy, Sligo Rep. E.S.B. and World Cup Champion for 1971.*

fishing in the vicinity of College Bay. Whatever wind we had was due West which meant that we were losing it as we came near the shore. However, as we commenced to drift out along the sand towards the deeper water the odd sedge was showing and in no time we saw a couple of fish moving. I covered one rising trout pretty fast, touched and lost him just as quickly.

Meanwhile Seán was into the first fish and playing him with as much skill as I have seen in all my days of angling. The Maguires are up there with the best of them, and Seán eventually brought a trout of over 1.5lbs to the net, this time to an olive bumble. We went back to the shore for another drift as we had the area to ourselves and with an occasional fish showing, we were not going anywhere. Next drift was more productive for Seán who put a nice 2 pounder with what he already had. It was still early and we decided to do a similar drift nearer the College. At this stage the wind was beginning to change. Sean covered another rising fish and "bang" he was in again. After some time he succeeded in netting another trout of at least 1.5lbs.

At this stage I was beginning to talk to myself and wondered why the fish were being selective or maybe, Maguire's flies were superior. Seán is an excellent Fly Tier, no doubt a skill he has acquired from his father, Denis and has now handed on to his son, Darren.

It was time to pull in for lunch, as the rise had stopped once the wind changed and it now seemed to die altogether and the sun broke through. We met a few more competitors at lunch time but they did not have any luck. It was at this stage that Sean showed me his Red and Green Peter Variant. I had not seen one like this before but when one was offered I gladly accepted and tied it on to top dropper. We commenced once more, this time fishing in almost the opposite direction as the light wind was coming across the lake and we were drifting in towards the shore. I will always remember the drift we did into College Bay, the sun shining behind us and the sky getting more cloudy. I cast into the shallow water and then as I slowly retrieved I saw him. A great big shadow moved out under the Maguire pattern and surfaced slowly. I still remember seeing the big red spots of what undoubtedly was a very big gillaroo as he came closer to the fly. In retrieving I was running out of space so I gently lifted off the flies and presented them once more in a shortened cast. Back he came again. This time I left the flies and he actually surfaced silently beside them, motionless for what seemed like a minute but in fact was only a second and then disappeared slowly. Did we come back again and again? Yes we did, but to no avail.

The day was still young, but no matter where we went after that and I can assure you that we visited some hot spots, we had no more action. Seán was a very popular winner that evening; his three fish weighed a good 5.23lbs and I count him among my friends from Lough Melvin where I enjoy my annual visit to Sonaghan Country towards the end of August each year. In 2nd place that year was Brendan Smith from Sligo, also a former winner with a single fish of 4.13lbs and third was Ronnie Law also from Northern Ireland with 3 fish weighing 4.03lbs.

As already stated Matthew Kennedy had the Heaviest Fish that year and also came 4th, undoubtedly a remarkable feat for an angler who was not in good health at the time and who regrettably is now no longer with us. Cyril Murray, Galway won the Thursday heat with 3 fish weighing 5.88lbs; Matt Kennedy on Friday with 2 fish for 8.56lbs; Matthew Higgins, Galway on Saturday with 2 fish weighing 4.71lbs and on Sunday, Oliver Walsh with 2 fish weighing 4.49lbs. Madeline Kelly, Islandmagee, Co. Antrim, won the Best Lady Angler category in what undoubtedly was the most successful World Cup competition to date. Best Junior angler of the competition was Patrick Mettler, Belleek, Co. Fermanagh. Main Sponsors to the competition this year were Caidéil M.P. Teoranta and the ESB, and a boat trailer was added to first prize of Boat, Engine and Crystal Cut Glass Trophy sponsored as usual by Martin Murphy, Main St., Ballinrobe to commemorate the 25th staging of the event under the Ballinrobe banner. Burke Boats sponsored a 19ft Anglers Fancy Boat for the lucky Heaviest Fish category winner. The predominant name on the winning team that year was Molamphy with Tom, Christy, and Martin teaming up with Matthew Kennedy. Overseas winner was Omer De Ridder, Belgium.

## 1993 – Fishery Board Staff Member Wins World Cup

Administration associated with the selection of the team prize was proving difficult, partly because the same anglers were being nominated on different teams and it was agreed reluctantly around this time to dispense with this prize. Geoff McDonald took over as Chairman of the organising committee with Ray Owens as Secretary and Liam Horan reported in the *Western People* that "the manner in which this competition has grown in recent years has taken the organisers by surprise".

This was the 26th event run by the Ballinrobe Committee, but if one adds on the 12 years of competition run by the Castlebar Club prior to this it was the 38th running of the event. The competition was now estimated to be worth £250,000 to the local economy in addition to being a marketing tool of great value for the extended season. Main sponsors for the competition in 1993 in addition to Burke Boats were McHale Engineering Ltd and the ESB.

Conditions during the competition were quite windy especially during the last 2 days and 570 anglers caught 371 fish weighing 453.63lbs. in 713 rod days. The results show that Frank Reilly of the Western Regional Fisheries Board, a

*Chairman Geoff McDonald presents World Cup to 1993 Winner, Frank Reilly.*

native of Loughrea, but living in Cong at the time won the competition "going away from the field" with Brian Joyce of Derrypark, owner of the award winning self catering premises on the shores of picturesque Maamtrasna Bay once more as winning boatman. Frank had a catch of 4 trout weighing 8.29lbs. Frank was also Irish International Captain at the time.

In 2nd place was Noel Dwyer, a Leinster angler with 2 trout weighing 4.39 lbs and third was Terry McGovern, Garrison, Co. Fermanagh with 2 fish weighing 4.27lbs. In fourth place was Jim Dillon with 2 fish weighing 4.24lbs. If the weights of the first four are added up we get 10 trout weighing 21.19lbs or an average of 2.12lbs which supports my long standing theory that Mask fishes best in fresh wind conditions giving a good wave.

The Heat winners were; Frank O'Hara, Ballinrobe with 5 trout for 5.82lbs, Seán Hopkins, Castlebar 3 trout for 3.97lbs, Roy Ferguson, Cookstown, 3 trout for 3.81lbs and Gerard Lenihan from Cork who recorded 3 trout for 6.68lbs. The prize for the Heaviest Fish was won by Michael Stack with a weight of 5.45lbs and the best lady angler finalist once again was Madeline Kelly from Islandmagee, Co. Antrim with 3 fish for 2.57lbs. The best overseas angler was Peter Thomas, former English International Captain with 4 trout weighing 4.17lbs.

## 1994 – A Visit From Uachtarán na hÉireann

Anthony O'Malley-Daly writing in *The Sun* of Friday May 20th 1994 reported as follows; "It's the largest of its kind in Europe. Last year it attracted an entry of 570 anglers from Ireland, U.K. and the rest of Europe. Our President, Mary Robinson, will open this year's event at 10.30 am, 28th July, from Cushlough. What is it? Well, it's the 27th World Cup Trout wet fly angling championship to be held on Lough Mask, commencing with 4 heats from Thursday 28th July. The climax is the final to be fished on Monday 1st August. At the end of this fishing extravaganza the winner will receive the Perpetual World Silver Cup".

Marie Walsh took over as Secretary and proved to be extremely efficient and dedicated at her post. Geoff McDonald was Chairman with Tom Mulvey as Boat Manager. The Chairman introduced all Committee members to President Robinson who then officially opened the competition and started the first heat. In an excellent speech she quite rightly related the importance of angling, and trout fishing in particular, to the economy of Ireland and as a way of maintaining the purity of lakes such as Mask. A number of presentations were made to the President who then unveiled a plaque to commemorate the event.

Phil Brookes recalled his experience on the previous year for me. Often the fish will boil at the fly as if it has been waiting for it forever. On striking, one discovered that one is striking fresh air – the fish never took the fly and probably never intended to. A good pull underwater again signifies a fish but it has gone before the angler is even aware of its presence. Another good boil is observed and, simultaneously, the fish is felt as it feels the resistance of the rod and ejects the fly before the angler has hope of striking. All these, and many more other missed opportunities, await to test your skill, sense of humour, and blood pressure. Finally, long after hope has been abandoned, you meet yet another rise, apparently one just like all the others. But not quite. Unbelievably, the fish is hooked. It looks and feels like a good one, a pound and-a-half at least, and your whole world shrinks into a small slice of water within which swims your prize. The boatman makes a single sweep with the net and the fish is yours. You can't believe it, you will not let yourself believe it, but you have just qualified for the World Cup Finals!!

The statistics for the 1994 competition were that 602 competitors took part and caught 259 trout weighing 316.44lbs in 753 rod days, with an average weight of 1.22lbs in variable to fine weather conditions.

*Phil Brookes, Luton, makes a presentation to President Mary Robinson, on behalf of overseas anglers competing.*

*President Robinson Opens the 1994 World Cup*
*Denis Kelleher PRO, President Mary Robinson, Mr. N. Robinson and Main Sponsor John P. Burke, Burke Boats at Cushlough Bay, Lough Mask.*

In 1994 however, Phil acted as boatman on the final day and his two anglers were Derry Ryan from Carlow and Bobby Woods from Dublin. According to the forecast, the wind would die later in the day and, that should be the realistic end to their hopes and expectations. Phil's idea was simple enough. Instead of driving down the lake for miles, only to watch the last of the wind fade to nothing, he bravely decided to start the first drift as soon as they were outside Cushlough Bay, so saving precious time. The wake from the other boats could still be felt as the first casts were made. Bob stripped his flies under the surface on a sinking line while Derry was a top-of-the-water man and he brought the top dropper skimming across the waves. They drifted along the outer shore of Martins' Island when half way

*Derry Ryan, Carlow, 1994 World Cup Winner, with Geoff McDonald, Chairman.*

down the shore a fine trout rolled over his wet Mayfly and was firmly hooked. Barely a half an hour had passed and Phil had scooped a 2 pounder into the net. Derry took another fine trout of 1.25lbs to a nicely tied Murrough on the middle dropper at the outer edge of the island. Phil rightly advised Derry that another fish would do a lot for his chances but Derry replied that he was enjoying his day and another fish would be a bonus. Bob was also in good humour although fishless and they returned to Martins' Island for the lunch. The wind, despite the gloomy forecast looked like keeping up.

In the afternoon they moved on to fish around Devenish Island but had no success. They then decided to retrace their steps and go back to where they had started in the morning. Phil saw a great trout fire itself out of the water and crash back beneath the waves. He worked the oar to put the boat over the fish and describes how Derry was changing flies for the hundredth time that day and now changed to a Mayfly Nymph. They were now at the spot where the large fish had moved. The thought had barely registered when Derry lifted his rod and a great trout was hooked. The fish put up an admirable battle but eventually came to the net, almost 3lbs weight.

Derry Ryan from Carlow, now living in Dublin won the World Cup that year with 3 trout weighing 6.1lbs and in 2nd place was Andrew Doggart, Newtownards, Co Down with 3 fish for 2.89lbs and in third position was Denis O'Keeffe from Cavan with 2 fish weighing 2.5lbs. Jim Cooke from Edinburgh won the heaviest fish prize with 3.72lbs and the team prize that year was won by the Northern Ireland team of Brian Hallet, Ruth Mettler, Frankie McPhillips and Ignatius Roche with 7 fish weighing 8.67lbs. Overseas winner was the same Jim Cooke with 2 fish for 4.76lbs. There was a dead heat for the Ladies prize between two Irish team members, Mary Geary of Pontoon and Ruth Mettler, Belleek, Co Fermanagh, each weighing in at 3.35lbs. Best under 21 angler was Munster angler Shane Lancaster with 3 fish weighing 3.58lbs. Dublin angler Martin Kearney won Thursday's heat with 2 fish-4.58lbs, Seamus Eighan, Tyrrelspass, Westmeath won on Friday with 2 fish for 4.27lbs, Peter Donnan, Dunmurray, was the winner on Saturday with 2 fish for 3.99lbs and finally on Sunday, Martin Ferguson, Co Antrim with one fish weighing 2.65lbs.

## 1995 – The Wet Fly Dry Fly Controversy

The *Western People* of 29th April 1995 reported that there would be a large increase in the number of overseas anglers participating in the World Cup competition. Indications were that the greatest percentage increase would be anglers from the UK with a lesser increase from Northern Ireland. who already constituted one third of the entire entry. John Nestor, a Galway man and a keen angler now resident in Ballinrobe took over as chairman of the 1995 competition and announced that the entry had reached the 600 mark and that the production of a special colour brochure for the overseas market and excellent coverage in the Nov '94 edition of *Trout and Salmon* were responsible for this. Joining the main list of Sponsors this year was the "K Club" who agreed to sponsor a 19ft "Anglers Fancy" boat for the Heaviest Fish Category.

*Gerry Cairns, 1995 World Cup Winner, with John Nestor, Chairman.*

The 1995 World Cup Committee were as follows: President, Atty McCormack; Chairman, John Nestor; Secretary, Marie Walsh; Boat Manager, Tom Mulvey; and PRO, Denis Kelleher. Committee: Esther Sweeney, Robbie O'Grady, Jimmy Murphy, Joe Cusack, Michael Harnesse, Geoff McDonald, Dominic Curran and Ray Owens.

World Cup Champion for 1995 after a tough competition in Mediterranean conditions was Gerry Cairns of Caherdavin, Limerick, with 1 trout weighing 1.93lbs In 2nd place came former 2 time World Cup Champion local man Robbie O'Grady with 1 trout weighing 1.73lbs and third was North Western Regional Fisheries Board officer John Bourke from Ballina with 1 trout weighing 1.61lbs.

All boats were supplied with an adequate supply of drinking water courtesy of Michael Harnesse, Anchor Bar and Connacht Mineral Waters Co.

As the "Hat" rule applied on this year, meaning that anyone who qualified by means of the hat could only fish for from 4th prize downwards, the 4th prize winner, Paul Loscher, Dublin had 1 fish for 1.79lbs. Only 12 fish were caught in the final that year. The Heaviest fish prize went to Kevin Garn from Northampton with a trout in the Friday heat of 3.60lbs. Winner of the under 21 prize sponsored by Phil Brookes was Patrick Molloy with a trout of 2.24lbs in the Friday heat also. John Bourke of Ballina won the first heat with J.J. Malone as boatman on Thursday with a catch of 3 trout weighing 4.57lbs and the total catch that day although quite poor at 25 trout was the best return for the competition. On Friday Kevin Garn from Northampton who had Richie Brown as boatman won his heat with the heaviest fish of the competition at 3.60lbs. Saturday's heat was won by Gerry Cassidy with Ronan Cusack as boatman with 1 fish weighing 1.95lbs and finally on Sunday local veteran Robbie O'Grady won his heat with a trout weighing 2.15lbs.

Over 600 anglers competed in one of the finest August week-ends ever remembered on Lough Mask and as the final statistics show, the trout stayed on the bottom for most of the week-end. 620 anglers caught 80 trout weighing 113.62lbs in 775 rod days, an average of 1.42lbs.

One of the problems that had reared its head on a regular basis was that of drawing a distinction between the wet-fly and dry-fly fishing method of fishing for trout, both well-tried and tested angling methods. The impulse of a trout to attack anything which behaves unnaturally is well known. The trout can lie quietly on the lake bottom surrounded by all kinds of pupae or minnows, but let a winged dressing of a fly be pulled across his path in a totally unnatural way and he can be impelled to attack it. This is wet fly fishing as we know. However, Lake fishing with a team of three or four wet flies some of which are now so developed that they can be "bobbed" successfully from the top dropper which is kept in the skin of the surface and slowly lifted off for another cast. Some flies are even lightly treated to help them float and it is when this happens that the barriers start tumbling down between wet and dry fly fishing.

It is true that Dry Fly fishing generally takes place when the fish are rising and the angler seeks to imitate the natural fly on the surface. Oh! for those long evenings following a summer flood on the Upper Fergus in Co. Clare, with the blue-winged olive hatch. However, I have also seen anglers fishing dry fly without a rise in sight and still getting the odd trout especially on the lake surface. The various points of view were argued regularly at the Committee table and eventually because the matter was getting extremely difficult to police, we decided to drop the word "Wet" and simply call the competition a Trout Fly competition but still insist that not less than 2 and not more than 4 flies can be used in any cast. This change did not occur until 1996.

## 1996 – Another McLoughlin

A Press release dated the 26th of June stated the first entry for the World Cup competition of that year had arrived in Ballinrobe from Pente, Arizona. The value of first prize was now estimated to be £2,500. John P. Burke of Burke Boats and Kevin Duffy, the well known Johnson Agent from Headford had teamed up with Martin Murphy, Newsagent, Ballinrobe for many years to sponsor this prize. All sponsors were invited to a launch of the event that year and it was a

*Chairman, John Nestor, presents the World Cup to 1996 Champion Noel McLoughlin, Kells, Co. Westmeath. On left J. P. Burke, on right Martin Murphy (Sponsors).*

matter of great satisfaction that we now had a good mix of sponsorship, both local and not so local supporting the competition.

Former Secretary Tony Mulloy and former Treasurer, our life President the late Attie McCormack got special mention for their sterling work over a long period of years on behalf of the competition and the importance of game angling to the local tourism economy was stressed.

Gowan & Bradshaw of Galway sponsored third prize that year and local subscribers and business interests combined to sponsor a 19ft fibre glass boat for the Heaviest Fish Prize and Biggins Corner Bar sponsored a substantial prize for the best competing member of Ballinrobe & District Anglers.

Kells in Co. Meath had registered 2 World Cup wins in 1987 and 1991 and this year would provide a third winner from the Royal County with Noel McLoughlin, a brother of Hughie who won in 1987. With a catch of 2 trout weighing 4.69lbs and boatman Joe Conroy from Brownstown. Noel pipped another Kells World Cup champion of 1991 into 2nd place. Brendan Moran had one large trout weighing 4.44lbs; he had won the 1991 competition with a trout of 3.95lbs and was now establishing a reputation for himself as someone who could catch a big fish at the right time.

In third place that year was Pádraig O'Brien with another good trout of 4.26lbs. Winner of the Heaviest Fish category that year was Frank Hone from Dublin with a beautiful trout of 7.75lbs and his boatman was Martin Groonell. Frank also won the Sunday heat with this fish which is the best trout I've seen weighed in this competition. Best overseas angler was Phil Brookes from Luton with 2 fish for 2.072lbs. Best lady Angler was Gráinne Kelly of that famous Kelly family of anglers from Cloghans, Ballina with trout weighing 5.32lbs. Joe Conroy was the boatman who brought in the winner and the best boatman of the competition was Martin Groonell with a combined weight of fish to his boat at 17.74lbs. Gráinne Kelly also won the Thursday heat with 3 for 5.32lbs and with Joe Crean as boatman Jimmy Molloy won on Friday with boatman Bill Colohan and a catch of 2 fish for 3.67lbs and on Saturday former World cup champion Derry Ryan won with Michael Farragher as boatman with a catch of 4 fish weighing 5.66 lbs. 620 anglers competed in the 1996 World Cup and caught a total of 329 trout weighing 446.97lbs

## 1997 – Year of Change

Paul McCormack in an article in the December issue of *Trout and Salmon* wrote about enjoying some highly unexpected sport in Lough Mask's no-man's land. Indeed, stories were spreading around of some remarkable catches of trout taken in areas which had not been fished heretofore. These areas were mainly in the much deeper water stretching from north to south and the fishing was completely different in so far as one could drift for half a mile before meeting a fish. The trout in common with their surroundings are of a darker colour and inclined to shoal and feed mainly on daphne. One could draw a comparison with the Sonaghan of Lough Melvin because their natural habitat looks the same, and they explode into life when hooked in a similar way, but the Mask fish average about 1.25lbs and their tails would not be as powerful as the Sonaghan, which seems to have a tail slightly out of proportion with the rest of its body and this no doubt accounts for its great fighting qualities. At any rate boats were beginning to visit Lough Mask's "No-man's land" more regularly and were having more success at this time. Some efforts were being made to keep the secret but in the relaxed atmosphere of the Ballinrobe angling pubs at night one could learn enough to become extremely suspicious about the new "hot spots". The difficulty was that the majority of Lough Mask's surface is more than 15 feet deep and these dark trout liked to move around. The very presence of these fish was arousing everyone's curiosity and questions were being asked as to whether this was not some other species of trout who were feeding on daphne for years or was it simply that the fish whose normal habitat was in the shallows had for some reason deserted the shallows and now resided in the deep also changing their feeding habits? The Fishery Board assure me that there is no evidence to suggest that

*World Cup 1997 Champion, Pádraig Munroe, Partry, with Mattie Cusack, winning Boatman.*

these deep water trout are a separate species, and I have already noticed that the numbers of trout caught in some areas of Lough Mask e.g. The "Rocky Shore" area is greatly reduced. If fish who previously frequented the shallows, now reside in the deeper water what has changed to cause this?

The 1997 Season was one of the better years for anglers on Lough Mask and it fished extremely well even before the May Fly season. A two day competition run by Ballinrobe & District Trout Anglers had 68 anglers competing on Lough Mask over 2 days, 3rd and 4th of May and caught 123 trout weighing 173lbs. Denis J. Cronin, Kenmare, Co. Kerry won with 10 trout for both days weighing 11lbs 12.5ozs. 2nd was Tom Sweeney, Macroom, Co Cork with 5 trout weighing 9lbs 10.5ozs and 3rd was another Denis Cronin, this time from Cork with 4 trout weighing 8lbs 8.75ozs.

The Ballinrobe Club was getting involved in major development work and had plans to erect a Hatchery on the Bulkaun River. Proceeds from a number of competitions would go to defray some of the expense.

The 1997 Lough Mask World Cup lived up to all the expectations of the previous competitions and some boats were observed drifting in strange places, but "No Mans Land" was not automatically changing into "The Promised Land" for everyone.

Thursday's heat results are not available and John E. Byrne had a catch of 5 trout weighing 10.28lbs to win Fridayís heat with something to spare. On Saturday which was a brighter day, Terry Walsh had 2 fish weighing 5.59lbs to win the heat with Cavan man Denis O'Keeffe as boatman. 1995 World Champion Gerry Cairns from Limerick showed that he had not lost his touch when he won Sunday's heat with 5 fish weighing 8.76lbs and Seán Maloney as boatman. Padraic Munroe from Partry was drawn with Larry Poynton and local boatman Mattie Cusack. Padraic is a keen angler and had been studying this new phenomenon of trout moving in deep places. Mattie motored for the deep water near Carraiginmeanlach and the Rocky Shore that morning and at 12 .30 Padraic had 3 trout in the boat. No Man's Land was turning into the "Promised Land" for him.

However this was followed by a spell of splashing fish who were not interested in getting hooked. At some stage later the magic bottle was produced and a drop of whiskey had a calming effect on proceedings. Padraic who fished with Bumble Olives and the old reliable Green Peter which I suspect may have had some new clothes on commenced to build on his earlier catch of 3.

On Monday evening Padraic Munroe was crowned 1997 World Champion with a catch of 6 trout weighing 8.84lbs with Mattie Cusack as boatman and in 2nd place was 1986 World Champion Brian Hallett, Belleek, Co. Fermanagh with 5 fish weighing 6.92lbs. Paul Heraty from Lanesboro had the 3rd best weight at 6.75lbs but had qualified out of the "Hat" so he was relegated to 4th and John Reidy with 4 fish weighing 6.03lbs won 3rd prize. The heaviest fish category in 1997 was won by David O'Connor, Ballinrobe with a trout of 4.08lbs.

Our Patron Monsignor Tom Shannon had made the acquaintance of Cecil Johnson of Wyndways Farm, Flint Hill, Stanley, Co Durham, who had become none other than Baron Johnson of Kilmaine. The Baron, who had shown a great interest in the old Barony, became a regular visitor and benefactor at Primary School level in the area and had shown an interest in many aspects of local life, including horse racing and fishing. He sponsored a silver rose bowl annually for the best World Cup angler from the Barony from 1997 on, and the first winner of this prize was David O'Connor. Stephen Kidd of Bonnyrigg, Scotland won the best overseas angler prize and Brian Thomas of Cumbria was 2nd in this category. Roseanna Hanley won the Lady's prize and best boatman over the competition in addition to winning boatman on the final day was Mattie Cusack who had a great competition.

Total number of anglers was 530 and the total no of fish caught were 463 weighing 726.2lbs in 662 rod days with an average weight of 1.568lbs.

# 1998 – A Successful Boat manager

*Craig Murray, Ballyclare, Co. Antrim, presented with 1998 World Cup by Ray Owens, Chairman.*

Tom Mulvey as Boat Manager was pushing out the frontiers as never before and any regular angler on Lough Mask regardless of where he was from was being recruited as a potential boatman for the competition provided he had the proper equipment and experience of the lake. Tom got great co-operation from the anglers in his unenviable task and this enabled further expansion of the competition. He also established himself as a very important link in the development of a software programme which guaranteed a continuation in the high standards of competition management and presentation of results over the years. 1998 was destined to be no exception.

## Tourism Angling Measure Plan

However, the whole area of fisheries development was not without its own difficulties at this time. The problems resulted from suspension of the Tourism Angling Measure Development Plan. Some Pike and coarse angling interests were objecting to certain aspects of the plan, mainly those dealing with predator control. Over 300 Anglers, Tourism providers and other interests attended a public meeting at the Railway Inn, Ballinrobe in early March chaired by Tom Byrne who was also chairman of the federation of angling clubs around Lough's Mask and Carra. Tom very quickly outlined the problems in detail and called for a complete restoration of the original development scheme including the culling of pike on Lough Mask. Mr Byrne stated that there were 367 pike angling lakes in the country and a number of these were in Co Mayo already, in compari-son to only 11 major wild brown trout fisheries throughout the country.

In attendance at the meeting were Deputy Cooper-Flynn, who stated that she would be looking for answers from the chief executive of the Central Fisheries Board to a number of questions that had arisen.

Deputy Jim Higgins stated that "suspension of the development of a natural resource as important as Lough's Mask or Carra was an absolute disgrace and he would be asking questions about this in Dáil Éireann in the following few days."

Senator Frank Chambers undertook to facilitate a meeting between the Minister for the Marine Dr Michael Woods and the Committee at an early date. Clubs from as far away as Dundalk, Dublin, Drogheda, Athlone, Cork, Galway, Roscommon and individuals from all over the Country attended and many expressed their anger at the level of interference taking place.

President of the Trout Anglersí Federation of Ireland, representing 18,000 anglers, John P. Burke outlined the difficulties his organisation had in communicating with the Dept of The Marine and stated that all trout angling clubs North and South were prepared to back this campaign for the restoration and full implementation of the developement plan on Mask and Carra. The Committee did eventually succeed in getting a hearing with the Minister and the plan was reinstated.

Meanwhile, angling for this year was proving quite good and Oughterard anglers dominated a 2 day Trout Fly Competition held by Ballinrobe & District Trout Anglers on Lough Mask on the 2nd and 3rd May. 82 anglers competed and 154 trout weighing 228.3lbs or an average of 1.48lbs over the two days. Michael Faherty, Oughterard was 1st with 12 trout for the 2 days weighing 16.41lbs. Patrick Molloy, also from Oughterard was 2nd with 9 fish weighing 13lbs.35 and third was Oughterard man Tom Kelly with 6 trout weighing 8.99lbs.

On the 23rd of June a Press Release indicated that one third of the total entry for the World Cup came from Northern Ireland and that England, Scotland and Wales were also well represented annually. A smaller group of anglers from mainland Europe also compete in what has developed to be one of the most popular and certainly the largest event of its kind that this country has seen. Despite some good early season fishing, Lough Mask reported a very poor May Fly season and catches generally had been light. However, this followed a similar pattern to 1997, which if carried through, should see an improvement in trout fly angling from late July onwards.

**John P. Burke – A Generous Sponsor**

John P. Burke served as PRO for the competition from 1976 to 1981. He took over from Tony Mulloy as competition secretary in 1981 and continued in that capacity until 1986. John Paddy has served as Chairman of both the Connaught Angling Council and Trout Anglers Federation of Ireland and followed with a period as PRO of T.A.F.I. He was recently elected as Chairman of T.A.F.I. for a second term, the only one to achieve this distinction, and is a member of the Board of the Western Regional Fisheries. A boat builder by trade, he has inherited great skills and is continuously modernising and adding to his "Angler Fancy" range of fibre glass lake boats for the home and overseas markets. As the main sponsor to the competition, he had fully sponsored 21 top of the range boats to date for the World Cup winners and played a huge role in the success of the event. More importantly he has generously given of his time in the interests of Irish angling at Connacht Council and National level and only recently became the only man to be elected as Chairman of T.A.F.I. for a second term. His late father is listed among the sponsors of the Inaugural World Cup in 1953.

Martin Murphy, another very committed community activist with "Lake District Enterprise", Ballinrobe Town Traders and very prominent in the local GAA Club had also recognised the value of the World Cup Competition to the area at an early stage and became the annual sponsor of the Galway Crystal Cut Glass Trophy. Kevin Duffy, the well known Johnson Outboard Agent from Headford, Auctioneer, Angler, Artist and Writer to name just a few of his interests had negotiated special sponsorship arrangements for three of the larger competitions including the World Cup, and he was also joined by the *Mayo News* from where some of the information for this publication originated, and these were the four main sponsors of the competition at this time. We had a host of smaller sponsors who also played a major role in sponsorship and as a result of their generosity it was possible to increase the committee contribution towards fishery development, which was becoming closely linked with stream enhancement through gravelling and local Trout Hatchery developments.

Lough Mask fished very well during the 1998 competition and, indeed the cut-off point for qualification in the 4th heat at 3.1lbs was one of the highest on record if one discounts the 1980 "Year of the Stockies". Fish were caught in deep and shallow water and boats were seen drifting in very unusual places once again. Traditional fly patterns were reported as getting the best results. Among them, Bibios, Daddy Long Legs, Dabblers of all kinds and of course, Green Peters got special mention. Weather conditions contributed greatly to the success of the competition.

The 1998 champion came from Northern Ireland, namely Craig Murray of Ballyclare, Co. Antrim with a catch of 2 trout weighing 8.62lbs, and in 2nd place was Patrick Molloy of Oughterard with 4 fish weighing 6.53lbs. Third was Martin McGorian of Walkinstown, Dublin with 5 fish weighing 6.41lbs. The Heaviest Fish Prize of a 19ft anglers Fancy Boat went to Michael Mason, Carrick on Shannon, Co Leitrim with a trout of 5.27lbs. Best under 21 angler was James Kelly from Oughterard with a catch of 5 fish weighing 6.01lbs, and the best Lady

Angler was Mary Feerick, Ballinrobe with 3 fish weighing 6.67lbs. Best overseas angler was Phil Brookes of Luton with 3 fish weighing 7.31lbs. The Boatmens' prizes were awarded as follows: John Wilkinson who brought in the overall winner, Bert Cory 2nd and Harald Schmitt 3rd, and a special prize was awarded to Joe Cusack who had an overall weight of 25.21lbs of trout to his boat during the competition. Heat results were as follows: Thursday – Basil Shields, Oughterard – 5 trout for 7.99lbs. Friday – John R. Forde, Northern Ireland – 6 trout for 7.82lbs Saturday – Colin Wilson, N.I. – 4 trout for 6.49lbs. Fechin McMorrow from Collooney, Co Sligo won the Sunday heat with a catch of 5 fish weighing 10.51lbs. 150 anglers caught 177 trout for 291lbs in excellent weather conditions during that heat. Once again a record breaking 548 anglers competed over the competition and weighed in 642 trout for 975.31lbs in 685 rod days, giving an average of 1.52lbs.

## 1999 – Generous Sponsors

With Joe Cusack as Chairman the 32nd World Cup organised in Ballinrobe was announced for July 29th to August 2nd. Entries to be with the Secretary, Esther Sweeney by 15th of July. However if we add on the 12 years under Castlebar Anglers' administration, 1999 would in fact be the 44th occasion that the competition had taken place.

The new "Anglers Fancy Supreme" boat by Burke Boats was fitted with swivel survival seats, extra buoyancy, a fibre glass non slip floor and was the ultimate in safety and comfort for the angler and made the 1st prize in this competition really special. Paul Duffy presented the 9.9 two stroke Johnson Outboard engine as usual and at this stage, as a result of increased sponsorship 16 prizes were on offer in addition to the host of special category prizes which have built up over the years for the final day.

Billy Burke, Anthony McCormack and Noel Finlay joined the Committee at this stage and the continuity of family involvement was guaranteed as Noel's late father Edwin and Uncle John were very involved in organising boats for the early World Cup competitions and Anthony was a nephew of our life President and long time Treasurer, Attie McCormack.

The World Cup Championships are well advertised in the immediate vicinity of Ballinrobe with banners and flags heralding the event. Most anglers will be greeted either in the pub or at the petrol station or shop with the same questions. Did you qualify? When are you fishing? Indeed I have reports of visitors to the town who may never have seen Lough Mask asked these questions, so good is the awareness among the local community that the Competition is underway and as sure as many of the "homer" anglers depart, many having to come to terms with the fact that they need to wait for another year before an opportunity to qualify will present itself again, another flush of competitors hit the town and eagerly explore the pubs for news of that day's heat. What did he catch them on?, Was she using floating or intermediate line? Tall tales and true are recounted and the grey area in between can become greyer than the waves of Lough Mask the next morning as the siren sounds at Cushlough to herald the start of another heat.

Sixty seven boats departed Cushlough Bay at 11am on Thursday 29th of July. In spite of bright sunny conditions 61 trout were caught and Mark Colton won the heat with 4 fish weighing 6.03lbs. The next heat on Friday 30th was one of those days that would be described as an angler's nightmare, calm and sunshine without a cloud in the sky and 126 competitors were lucky to account for 18 trout. Jim O'Callaghan from Partry struck lucky when he made contact and in due course netted a trout of 4.24lbs. Needless to say this fish won the heat for Jim and the 17 others who weighed in qualified in addition to a further 14 names from the "hat". Mediterranean like conditions prevailed for Saturday with a blazing sun all day and local chemists and supermarkets did a roaring trade in "Sun Block" or "Factor Cream" as anglers sought to defend themselves from the dreaded sunburn. Despite this heat winner Patrick Carson recorded 4 trout for a weight of 9.99 lbs which was truly amazing given the conditions that prevailed. A total of 92 boats departed Cushlough for the final heat on Sunday, but some prayers were answered because the weather changed and wet windy weather returned. I have often noticed that a sudden change from warm fine to more favourable conditions does not necessarily bring fish feeding again, perhaps water temperature is still too warm, however the catch that evening was not greatly improved, with 184 anglers weighing in 74 trout and Dara Tuohy winning the day with 4 trout weighing 5.81lbs.

The Bank Holiday Monday was blessed with a good wind, scattered cloud and a little sunshine. 158 anglers set off to fish in the final, but many of them, having qualified from the hat were not fishing for the top three prizes. Of the 158 who set out 70 weighed in fish and the heaviest catch on that day was the catch of local man David O'Connor with 4 trout weighing 5.85lbs. Unfortunately for David, his qualification was by means of the dreaded "Hat", and consequently his catch was relegated to 4th position. I had seen this happen before, and while the "rule" seemed fair at time of drafting, the worst possible scenario had unfolded with the relegation of David's catch. "Murphy's Law" had come home to roost once again.

"From Banbridge town in the County Down" came Billy Graham with 3 good trout for 5.40lbs followed by Feichin McMorrow Snr from Colooney, Co Sligo with 2 fish for 5.24lbs and Shannon Clements, Bunnamadden, Co Sligo in

*Chairman Joe Cusack; Sponsors Martin Murphy and J. P. Burke present the 1999 World Cup to Billy Graham, Banbridge, Co. Down.*

third place with 3 fish weighing 5.14lbs. The closeness of those 4 weights underlines the importance of having a digital scales properly calibrated for the weigh in. Eddie Hynes from Circular Rd, Limerick won the boat for the heaviest fish with a catch of a trout weighing 4.72lbs.

Winner of the Overseas prize that year was Brian Thomas, UK with 3 fish for 5.50lbs and he won a one week angling holiday on Lough Mask, courtesy of Tom and Mary Feeney, Lakeshore Holiday Homes and a £200 travel voucher, compliments of "Irish Ferries". The best Junior Angler was Jonathan Tormey from Co. Meath who also won an array of prizes, the Perpetual Shield and personal Replica with an "Angling Book" sponsored by Phil Brookes, a box of Rogan Flies from that famous house in Ballyshannon and a fishing rod sponsored by Billy Burke, "Outdoor Pursuits", Ballinrobe.

Over the years sponsored prizes were also added for the best competitor from each Province and best local angler, and also to 2nd best in some of the major categories. The crucial role played by boatmen was also recognised and sponsored prizes were on offer from local Service Stations and Retailers. Corkman Frank Doyle was the winning Boatman on the final day in 1999 and Seamus O'Dare was the Boatman who brought in the heaviest catch over the competition.

Michael Kennedy, Manager of Western Regional Fisheries Board officiated at the final dinner and spoke on the ongoing stream development Total returns for the competition were as follows; an all time record of 626 anglers participated and weighed in 290 trout weighing 449.04lbs in 783 rod days.

The World Cup Committee met later that year to make special plans for the "Millennium Competition" and a decision was made to have an addition to first prize and a special "Angling Journalists" prize for the occasion. A special Crystal Globe was commissioned from Waterford Glass to mark the Millennium.

*The Millennium World Cup Globe.*

# Chapter 6
# To the Present and the Future

## 2000 – The Millenium Competition

On New Year's Day Ballinrobe & District Trout Anglers under the chairmanship of John Nestor gathered at Cushlough with their friends for a celebration of the first sunset of the new Millenium. There were special poetry readings to commemorate the occasion by Fr Peter Hughes, Jimmy Murphy and Bridie Mulloy, a plentiful supply of wine and the evening concluded with a sing-song and fireworks display as the sun set for the first time in 2001. A report in the "Trout Anglers Federation" annual newsletter on this celebration suggested that everyone had a great evening and people were already looking forward to the next one on New Year's Day 3001 !!!

### "Sunset – 2000"

by Bridie Mulloy

*"Sink, sink Millenium sun*
*Bring down sabre, bomb and gun.*
*Rise anew to a tranquil day,*
*With hopeful peace, a shining ray.*
*We've had our share of blood and tears*
*Throughout your thousand pox-marked years,*
*So sink the lot while we stand and cheer*
*And drink red wine at Cushlough pier".*

Monsignor Tom Shannon, Former Secretaries, Tony Mulloy and John P. Burke at the launch of 2000 Competition.

Jimmy Murphy, President of the Committee and an original founder member, angler, boatman, a great man to sing a song, sometimes a poet and always a lover of Lough Mask recited his poem describing "Lough Mask's Rocky Shores" on that memorable evening at Cushlough also.

## Extract from "Lough Mask's Rocky Shores"

by Jimmy Murphy

*"Where the fishermen stray,*
*They're on their way*
*Through shallows a' peeping all round*
*And the bobbing mayfly*
*The brown trout and I,*
*They can hear that quick splashing sound*
*Where the mountains stand near*
*And the Wild Geese appear*
*Where the birds fill their nests on the isles*
*Oh how I long o'er and o'er*
*To be back there once more*
*To walk on Lough Mask's rocky stiles.*

The World Cup Millenium competition was launched in Carney's Bar, Ballinrobe on Thursday evening the 23rd of July. A number of special features were added including 21 prizes of the final day and the competition dates were Thursday August 3rd to Monday, August 7th inclusive. The value of first prize was increased to in excess of £5,000 for the very first time and Burke Boats in association with McCarthy Insurance of Cork sponsored a special prize for the best Angling Journalist of the competition.

The chairman of the World Cup Committee Joe Cusack, who was only a 16 year old boatman when he boated the winner in 1957 offered a special welcome to all participants whether native, Northern Irish or overseas, to Ireland's lake district that August. A total number of 605 anglers came to Cushlough for the Millenium competition and the weather for that week-end was probably the best angling weather the competition has experienced since 1953. As a result the catches were particularly good and very little separated the main prize winners on Monday. Outstanding flies for this particular competition included such patterns as the Green Peter, Murrough, various may fly patterns, Green Dabblers, Olive Bumbles and a relative newcomer called the "Octopus" and the fish were moving on the surface throughout the competition.

Committee of World Cup 2000
*Back row (l. to r.): Noel Finlay, Tom Mulvey, Dominick Curran, Anthony McCormack, Joe Cusack, Robbie O'Grady.*
*Front row (l. to r.): Billy Burke, Jimmy Murphy, Denis Kelleher, Esther Sweeney, Ray Owens, Michael Harnesse.*

## The Competition of the Long Drifts

Any trout fisherman who was watching the action on Lough Mask from the Tourmakeady shore during the competition must have wondered if the boatmen of Lough Mask had gone completely mad because most of the traditional drifts were abandoned and many boats were seen drifting from the Tourmakeady shore straight across the lake but more particularly towards the Northern end. This trend continued throughout the heat-days of the competition and the stories were of fish caught in the deep water. The conditions obviously suited the Daphne feeders. The first heat on Thursday 3rd of August was won by Basil Bell, Chanterhill, Enniskillen with a catch of 5 fish weighing 7.65lbs. Basil's boatman was David O'Connor. Again with excellent conditions on Friday Michael McKiernan, Coosan, Athlone, who had 6 fish weighing 8.41lbs won the heat with boatman Mike Hamrogue. On Saturday it was the turn of Frank Reilly, Headford, a former World Cup Champion with an excellent catch of 9 trout weighing 13.29 lbs and Frank's boatman was Galway man Harold O'Toole.

I remember fishing in this heat with Kathleen Feerick as partner and boatman Niall Cusack. I had mixed feelings about these long drifts. However those feelings were very quickly put behind me as we both rose fish at the start. Niall drifted all

*Chairman Joe Cusack; Sponsor John P. Burke; World Cup Millennium Winner, Derry Ryan, Carlow and Martin Murphy, Sponsor.*

the way to the far shore near Ballygarry in a good south westerly wind and Kathleen quickly opened a commanding lead. We both saw plenty of action during the day and indeed it was well into the afternoon before I caught a fish and we both qualified comfortably although I hasten to add that Kathleen was after 5 fish, slightly more comfortable than I. The 4th and final heat was fished in slightly finer conditions and was won by David Stinson, Dreann, Kesh, Co. Fermanagh with 3 fish weighing 5.16lbs and the stage was set for the Milennium final on Monday 7th August.

The big question was whether this competition would be won on what now were becoming the standard long deep water drifts across the lake or whether the Bays and more traditional drifts would reassert themselves. As I exited the bay at the start of the competition with Galway Boatman Kenny O'Toole and the other competitor John Carson, I gave my recommendation to Kenny to have a go at Maamtrasna Bay. This was a considerable distance away and I think Kenny would have preferred to do some deep water fishing as it had paid off for him already in the heats. However, Kenny brought us to Maamtrasna and we both had a tremendous days fishing taking 9 trout between us and having a few misses as well. I hooked and broke in a good fish at the mouth of Maamtrasna that day, but then I doubt that I was the only one who had the big opportunity. One man had and certainly took it.

The record shows that Derry Ryan, Clogrennan Lime, Carlow, a financial controller with Roadstone created history by joining local well known angling specialist Robbie O'Grady and becoming only the 2nd man to win the coveted World Cup for the 2nd time with a catch of four trout weighing 7.51lbs. In 2nd place with 3 trout of the exact same weight was Belfast Bank Manager, Seán Irvine. Rule 11 states that when two or more anglers have equal weights of fish, the competitor with the greatest number of fish is deemed to be the winner.

The five trout which I caught weighed in at 7.34lbs were placed third and the Boat for the Heaviest fish of the competition was won by Derek McKenna with weight

*Chairman Joe Cusack presents the World Cup to 2000 Champion Derry Ryan, Carlow.*

of 4.83lbs. 4th and 5th prizes went to Peter McKenna, Sligo with 5 fish for 7.22lbs and 5th to Patrick Carson, Co. Down with 4 fish for 6.36lbs followed in 6th place by John Wilkinson, Drogheda with 3 fish weighing 6.30lbs in what was one of the closest finishes in the history of the competition. Only 1.21lbs separated 1st and 6th prizes. Best Lady Angler of the competition was Kathleen Feerick, Ballinrobe and best Overseas Angler was John McNamara, Ormiston, Scotland followed in 2nd position by Michael Shaw from Devon. Jonathan Morrissey won the "Under 21" category prize with a catch of 5 fish weighing 9.24lbs. Former champion Frank Reilly had the best heat catch and this earned him the prize for the best angler in the "Barony of Kilmaine" Richard Holmes was the Boatman who had the the best weight of fish over the competition, also brought in the winner on the final day and won both prizes. Other Boatmen to win prizes were: Pat McLoughlin, Vinnie O'Reilly and Kenny O'Toole.

There was a special cheer for 87 year old Tom Ketterick, Castlebar, now living in Ballina who qualified for the final. Overall statistics show that a total of 774 trout were caught in 757 rod days, weighing 1109.28lbs, an average of 1.43lbs and Saturday's Heat gave the greatest returns. 605 competitors took part. Undoubtedly Lough Mask produced some top class sport for the Millenium competition.

## 2001 – Foot and Mouth Casts a Shadow

Boatmen are always highly regarded on Lough Mask. Their knowledge of the Lake in all its moods has kept anglers safe and their up to date information on the movement or otherwise of trout has usually succeeded in bringing some measure of success to their competitors. One needs to be listening attentively to catch the stories and wit in some boats, whilst at the same time keep a certain level of attention focussed on one's flies. The unselfish attitude of the large number of anglers who agree to help out with the competition and forfeit a day or two of their own sport in order to help out by boating the competition is a huge contributing factor to its success. Without this commitment from the general body of anglers any amount of organising would not successfully run a competition of this size.

A cloud of uncertainty hung over the staging of the 2001 World Cup because of the rapid spread of the dreaded Foot & Mouth disease throughout the UK and into Northern Ireland. The Minister made an order banning all competitions on Friday 23rd March following an outbreak of the disease in Co. Louth and it looked as if all sporting events would fall for that year. However, that was as bad as it got. Following discussions with the relevant authorities the committee were advised on the 23rd of June that provided there were no further setbacks that it was safe to proceed with the competition. Esther Sweeney, chairperson of the Committee presented a cheque for £1,000 to John Nestor, chairman of Ballinrobe & District Anglers on 23rd of January towards costs of the Club's Hatchery in Ballinrobe. In addition to the promotion of Tourism it was now World Cup Committee policy to increasingly support any development work on spawning streams and hatcheries which would supplement the numbers of wild brown trout in the fishery.

Anthony McCormack moved into the position of Secretary of the competition and continued the long association of the McCormack family with the event, his uncle Atty was life President after spending a long term as Treasurer, a post that was now filled by Noel Finlay.

The competition itself proved once more to be highly successful, probably the best so far and 706 anglers competed with an overall catch of 506 trout in 883 rod days, weighing 720lbs in mixed weather conditions ranging from very calm to the more ideal breezy weather with showers. Nearly perfect conditions prevailed for the final on Monday 6th of August when Richard McDermott from Cloontrim, Co. Longford with a catch of 5 trout weighing 7.47lbs was awarded the World Silver Cup and the usual array of valuable prizes including 19ft Angler's Fancy Deluxe boat and 10hp Evinrude Engine and Crystal Glass Trophy. John Marshall of Ballynahinch, Co. Down took 4 trout for 6.60lbs to clinch the 2nd spot and a 9.9 2stroke Johnson and Harnesse Cup & replica. Third place went to another Ulster angler, Billy Graham, Banbridge, the 1999 winner with 4 trout for 6.28lbs and Jim Dillon from Donegal, won the Anglers' Fancy Lake Boat for landing the Heaviest Fish at 3.71lbs. Dr Phil Brooks from Luton won the overseas prize with 6 trout weighing 7.73lbs. Best lady angler was Mary Harkin, Dublin with 3 fish for 4.73lbs and best under 21 angler was Darren Reilly, Loughrea and the best

*Martin Murphy, Sponsor; John P. Burke (Sponsor); Richard McDermott, Cloontrim, Co. Longford, World Cup Champion 2001; Esther Sweeney (Hon. Sec.).*

angler in the Barony of Kilmaine was Pat Feerick. The four heat winners were Tom Sweeney, Cork, Sam Wilson and Freddy Steele from Northern Ireland and Patrick Kelly junior from Cloghans, Ballina.

The Boatman who brought in the winner on the final day was Frank Reilly, and Ronan Cusack won the prize for the boatman who brought in the Heaviest Fish of the competition.

Committee Chairperson, Esther Sweeney thanked all who contributed to the success of the event. The competition, with a considerable spin-off boosted the local tourism economy in a very positive way for the week. This competition got mention from a highly unusual source. The August edition of *HELLO* magazine covered the wedding of Pierce Brosnan and Keely Shaye Smith at nearby Ashford Castle and Ballintubber Abbey and referred to the fact that "Keely was held up in traffic on the way to her wedding – there were, after all, the World Angling Championships in nearby Ballinrobe and a regional soccer play-off that afternoon in Castlebar". *HELLO* got it right about the fishing in Ballinrobe but I doubt if the GAA authorities in Castlebar would be too impressed as Mayo were involved in an important Championship game.

## A "Shocking Experience"

Whist fishing with Jim Buchanan from Dalmellington, Ayreshire, after the competition near the southern shore at the back of Saints' Island we were both to experience the awesome power of electricity on the water following a short thunder storm. Jim is a more recent recruit to the World Cup competition but now competes annually with his son Jim Junior. As is recommended especially when using carbon fibre rods, we abandoned fishing for a time to enable the conditions improve. On our resumption we cast out the flies in the relatively calm conditions which then prevailed, when to our amazement the nylon casts and droppers lifted up from the water, and seemingly only remained anchored to the surface by the weight of the flies. All nylon remained suspended in the air and when we repeated the casts the same thing happened. Our mutual decision was to get out of the area as quickly as possible. That evening we related our experience to our angling colleagues but do not know whether they believed us or not!!

Our highly esteemed President, Attie McCormack, passed to his eternal reward on the 9th December after many long years of loyal service to World Cup Competition. Ar dheis Dé go raibh a hanam.

*From left to right: Robbie O'Grady; the late Attie McCormack, Life-President and long-serving Treasurer; and Jimmy Murphy – committee members since 1965.*

## 2002 – A Good Year for Partry Schoolteacher

The World Cup competition as presently constituted had peaked with 706 competitors in 2001 and commenced in 1953 with 164 competing anglers. From an organisational point of view the competition was recognised as a great success and the highest standards were maintained from the very beginning. Letters of thanks from satisfied anglers, many from overseas poured in each year and were a source of inspiration for the committee. One of the main priorities of the committee is to maintain a level playing pitch and placing of all competitors in boats has always been by open draw. It is now regarded as a fully-fledged festival and one third of our competitors come from Northern Ireland with smaller numbers competing from England, Scotland and Wales and a number from mainland Europe each year. Many competing anglers now stay in the Lough Mask area for 2 weeks and we always attract people who take the competition very seriously and there are also those for whom participation is everything. It is surprising how often they finish in the winners enclosure. Thankfully, the Western Lakes of Ireland are renowned as being among the best wild trout angling lakes in the world. That is still a fact, however long this fact remains is another matter.

Michael Harnesse resumed as Boat Manager for the 2002 competition and 673 anglers gathered at Cushlough Bay to compete in their nominated heats. Good angling weather was at hand on Thursday and David Dinsmore from Liverpool won the opening heat with a catch of 4 fish weighing an impressive 8.06lbs. There was good cloud cover for Friday's heat and Tom Sullivan, Galway won his heat. His catch included a trout of 4.85pounds which won the Heaviest Fish category prize of a 19ft boat on Monday evening.

The Saturday heat commenced amidst rising temperatures and fine weather, an angler's nightmare threatened once again. However the heat winner Philip McMahon, a Dublin schoolteacher caught 3 fish weighing 4.4 lbs to claim his place in the final. The final heat on Sunday was fished in hot, humid and sunny conditions and D.J. Byrne, Mountmellick, weighed in 2 fish to win the heat with a weight of 3.83lbs.

I remember qualifying for the final from the Saturday heat in very difficult conditions. I rose 2 fish in deep water and was lucky enough to get the first one.

The final on Monday was also a very difficult day with calm, almost flat conditions with temperatures soaring at times to 25 degrees. Perseverance and

*President Jimmy Murphy presents Julie Gerry, Maynooth, Co. Kildare with Lady Anglers Prize.*

*Martin Murphy, Sponsor; Esther Sweeney (Hon. Sec.); John P. Burke (Sponsor); Tom Byrne, World Cup Champion 2002; Brian O'Connor, Cong (Sponsor).*

skill with the dry fly paid off for the Chairman of the Federation of clubs around Loughs' Carra and Mask, Partry school principal Tom Byrne. Tom had already put days and hours of his time into Angling Federation business of all kinds, a conservationist and stalwart supporter of Game angling, he probably fine tuned his skills as an excellent dry fly angler on Lough Carra where he has achieved much success on those Summer evenings and later.

Tom succeeded with a catch of 3 trout weighing 6.39 lbs and won the acclaimed boat and engine with Crystal Glass and the World Cup. 2nd prize had a Banner County connection with Lawrence Hickey of Parteen taking the 9.9HP Yamaha Outboard engine for 3 fish weighing 4.10 lbs and Patsy Deery from Cootehill, Co Cavan came third with 2 fish for 3.52lbs. Top lady angler was Irish ladies fly fishing team captain Julie Gerry from Maynooth, Co Kildare and winning boatman was Junior McGahon. 673 anglers competed and total number of fish caught was 313 weighing 462.81lbs, giving an average weight of 1.48lbs, in 841 rod-days.

# World Cup Catches on Lough Mask since 1953

An examination of available data on trout catches from Lough Mask is interesting from many perspectives and the data in question have already been used and acknowledged by Central and Western Fishery Boards in some publications. In 1997 catches made during the World Cup were analysed by staff. The main findings were that trout growth in the lake was much higher than in the river, the majority of trout caught were 3 year olds or more and the oldest fish were 5 years going on 6.

The competitions of 1953, '54 and '55 took place over the Easter period, 1956 to '61 over Whit week-end, 1962 reverted to Easter and 1963 -'64 returned once more to Whit. Since 1965 the competition has taken place annually over August week-end with the exception of 1988, '89 and '90. The 10 inch limit applied to the World Cup from 1953 to approximately 1970 when the limit was increased on a voluntary basis to 12 inches. This became a legal limit with the introduction of a bye law in 1974 and was extended throughout the Corrib Mask catchment area. Unfortunately, weights are missing for a few years including 1953 but numbers of fish caught are available for every year except 1975. Figure

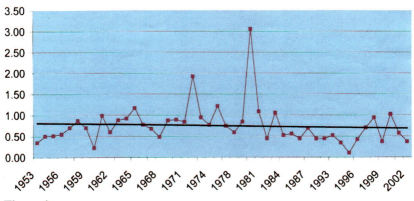

**Figure 1**

(1) shows the number of trout caught per rod-day over the history of the competition 1953 to 2002. Rod-days are defined by selecting the number of anglers who participated in the competition and adding the number of qualifiers who contested the final. The linear trend/regression line in this and other figures is used to calculate or predict a future value by using the existing values.

1980 recorded the highest catch per rod-day at 3.06, and the main reason for this was the widespread introduction of the "stockies" or farmed trout to Lough Mask as a compensatory measure for the arterial drainage scheme on the Robe and elsewhere which was ongoing at the time. If we eliminate 1980, the best recorded catch of wild trout from Lough Mask occurred during the competition of 2000 when 605 anglers caught 774 trout in 757 rod-days, an average of 1.02 trout per rod-day and the equivalent of a trout for every 11.5 hectares (28.4 acres) of water. The lowest recorded catch of 0.10 lbs per rod-day occurred in the August Bank Holiday weekend of 1995. The competition was fished against all the odds in a Mediterranean type climate during which sun block products were sold out and a plentiful supply of spring water was sponsored for each boat before departing the shore. Another point of interest is that although the lake got a three year rest from competition and general angling from 1988 to 1990,any corresponding improvement in wild trout stocks in the lake as a result of this was not reflected in catches when the competition resumed in 1991 and '92. The reverse was the case with an identical average catch per rod-day for both years of 0.44 lbs, a reduction from 0.56 lbs per rod-day in 1987. This would indicate that numbers of trout caught during the competition do not make any significant difference to

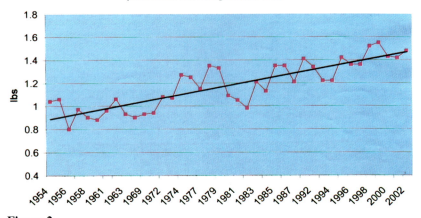

**Average weight of trout caught 1954-2002**
(with linear trend/regression line)

**Figure 2**

overall trout stocks in a 9,000 hectare lake of Mask's stature. The impact of the World Cup competitions since 1953 on the wild trout stocks of Mask can be further measured by calculating the average catch per competition between 1953 and 2002 which is 266 trout per annum or an average of one trout per 33.5 hectares (82.7 acres) of water.

Figure (2) shows that the general trend in average weights of trout caught over the lifespan of the World Cup competition has increased. The linear regression line indicates an increase from 1.04 lbs in 1954 to 1.48 lbs in 2002.

The average weight of trout caught peaked at 1.55 lbs in 1999 and the lowest average weight recorded was .80 lbs in 1956. A significant factor in figure (ii) was the increase in size limit for the competition from 10 inches to 12 inches, and this would automatically increase the average weight.

## No. of anglers (1953-2002)

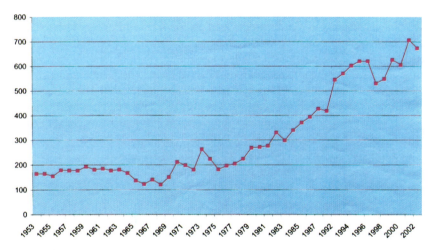

**Figure 3**

Finally figure (3) shows the increase in popularity of the event over the years. It commenced in 1953 with 164 competitors, dipped in 1966 to 122 and then grew steadily. The pace of growth accelerated in the 80s and 90s and peaked in 2001 with 706 competitors. This growth is largely attributed to the excellent administration of the competition over the years, attention to detail and the ability of boat managers to attract the large number of boatmen necessary. In more recent years Michael Harness and Tom Mulvey have filled the latter role and succeeded in attracting many of the competitors who already had a knowledge of the lake to act as boatmen for the increasing number of anglers participating.

## The Future

The immediate dangers to the continuation of the World Cup competition after 50 years are the spiralling costs of insurance in 2003 and the perception of the new Marine Safety Regulations among many boatmen. Whilst the latter difficulty may be resolved through negotiation it is difficult to see how the committee can continue to absorb the huge added insurance costs which, if handed on are going to greatly increase the cost of participation and perhaps, introduce the unwelcome label of being an elitist organisation, something that was not intended from the very start! How does one explain these extra insurance costs, having seen a competition take place and grow each year since 1953 without an insurance claim ? The insurance problem is not necessarily confined to angling events, but is now so great that it threatens the continued involvement of voluntary associations in the planning, administration and operation of many sporting and tourism events. We must not forget that many of these events bring much needed revenue to rural areas which may not otherwise benefit.

In conclusion it is comforting to read on *The Western People* of March 26th 2003, of good trout angling on Lough Mask. Billy Murphy of WRFB is quoted as being very pleased with fisheries development works on the streams and reports that more trout are now spawning in the catchment. The recent evidence of a continued existence of char in the lake would indicate that water quality is reasonably good at the present time. The fact that upgraded sewage treatment plants have now come on stream in Claremorris and Ballinrobe is a major bonus. However, a recent report from the WRFB highlights the consequences for salmonid fish in the River Robe and Lough Mask unless a major nutrient management initiative is undertaken. It also makes the point that 68 per cent of the Robe River surveyed is categorised as slightly or moderately polluted. Anglers and others throughout the Country have become far more conscious of where the lack of a coherent policy on water quality management may lead us. Angling clubs have become more involved in forming and operating Trout Hatcheries which can undoubtedly help with increasing trout populations but I feel that the long term sustainability of the great western lakes as major trout fisheries depends mainly on two factors. The guarantee of a water quality pure enough to support the salmonid species and an improvement in the suitability of our spawning rivers and streams to guarantee natural procreation. The most recent evidence of an improvement in trout population on the lake are the catches from a two day Development Competition held on the 3rd and 4th of May 2003 by Ballinrobe and District Trout Anglers Association. I was lucky enough to win the event with a catch of 16 trout weighing 10.12 Kilos followed in 2nd place by Martin Feerick with 14 trout weighing 9.21 Kilos and in third place Pat Feerick, Martin's brother with 13 trout weighing 8.23 Kilos.Those catches are as good as anything I have seen since I commenced fishing on Lough Mask.

One hopes that changes in agricultural policies, that are now taking place, will result in a land use which will be more appropriate to the nature of the soil and landscape and will allow life on both land and water to thrive. We would all like to think that in 50 years time the World Cup, perhaps with some changes, will continue to be fished on Lough Mask. However, in the words of Dr Phil Brooks from Luton, a regular World Cup competitor and lover of Lough Mask, " Unless the input of phosphates and nitrates to the waters of Loughs' Mask, Carra and Corrib is kept at low levels, these three gems known as the Corrib System will slowly but inevitably decline as one of the last major natural trout fisheries as others already have".

I am not in a position to produce statistics other than from World Cup catches, but like many others, I have also seen some disturbing changes and in the words of the well known Peter O'Reilly "personal observation is a good barometer – and much more painful."

*Towards Tourmakeady – "far away hills are green".*

*The views of some of our World Cup Visitors*

Bob Church (1979) – *The Trout Fisherman* – "Mighty Lough Mask in the west of Ireland is a water of many moods. Calm and placid one day, a quick change of weather can transform it. Mask can change from a placid inland sea into something rivalling the North Atlantic in a frighteningly short space of time. Its Boatmen are expert and although the lough has been their playground from boyhood they all treat Mask with the greatest respect. It was, Fred Cutler said, without any doubt at all the World's No 1 trout pond. I would hardly call 22,000 acres of the wildest water you've ever seen a pond, but I now believe all he says of Ireland's Lough Mask."

Phil Brookes (1994) – *Trout and Salmon* – "Possibly the most beautiful of the great lakes of the West of Ireland. The crystal-clear water, all 22,000 acres of it, allows a view of the massive submerged yellow rocks of limestone, some the size of houses."

Jim Buchanan (1998) – "Dapping with grasshoppers on Lough Carra, catching large wild trout on Lough Mask, missing a salmon on the turning fly and seeing wonderful large butterflies on an island on Lough Corrib, but most of all, the long hours talking fishing, drinking and song, will be with me throughout the winter months until I return to Ballinrobe."

*'Argument rages about the right moment to strike these big Irish Brownies'*
*– Phil Brookes* Trout & Salmon

## Early Records Lough Mask

Finally, I reproduce hereunder a number of articles and records first published to commemorate "An Tóstal" 1953 World Trout Fly Competition.

# AN TOSTAL, 1953.

# World Trout Fly Fishing Competition

UNDER THE AUSPICES OF

**CASTLEBAR AND DISTRICT TROUT ANGLERS' ASSOCIATION.**

Commencing Easter Saturday,
4th APRIL, 1953.

**VENUE—LOUGH MASK.**

Connaught Telegraph, Castlebar.

## WORLD TROUT FLY FISHING COMPETITION.

Oifig An Runai Pharlaiminte Don Aire Talmhaiochta
(Office of the Parliamentary Secretary to the Minister
for Agiculture),
3, Plas Chilldara,
(3, Kildare Place),
Baile Atha Cliath
(Dublin),
9 Eanair, 1953.

Tomas Uas. O Cuasail,
Ruai, Oinigh,
Cumann Slat Iascaire Breac Cheanntair
Caislean an Bharraigh,
Co. Mhuigheo.
A Mhic Ui Chuasail dhil,

  Glacaim buiochas leat as ucht me a chur ar an eolas i dtaoibh a bhfuil beartaithe ag an gComhlachas mar chabhair chun barr feabhais ar an Tostal 1953.

  Is ionmholta a bhfuil de eagraiocht agus de fhorbairt ar sport na slat-iascaireachta is feidir a chur i leith Comhlachas Chaislean a' Bharraigh.

  Ta meas agam ar an dea-obair ata deanta agus ata idir lamhaibh, agus taim sasta go mbeidh sport ar feabhas le fail ag cuairteoiri go ceanntar Chaislean a' Bharraigh le linn An Tostal faoi choinne comortas an Chomhlachais, agus ina theanta sin go mbeidh cead mile failte rompa ann.

  Mise, le caradas,
    GEAROID Mac PHARTHALAIN,
      Runai Parlaiminte.


Thomas Coucill, Esq.
Honorary Secretary,
Castlebar District Trout Anglers' Assoc.,
Castlebar,
Co. Mayo.
Dear Mr. Coucill,

  I thank you for informing me of the plans of your Association to help make An Tostal 1953 a success.

  The Castlebar Association has a creditable record in organising and developing the sport of angling.

  I commend the fine work done and in progress, and I am satisfied that An Tostal visitors to Castlebar district for the Association's Competition will be assured of good sport and a cead mile failte.

  Yours Sincerely,
    GERALD BARTLEY,
      Parliamentay Secretary.

## PRESERVING OUR HERITAGE.

(By MICHAEL KENNEDY, Secretary, Irish Fisheries Trust, Dublin).

IN placid lowland river and rushing hill stream, in mountain lough, and in the big lakes of the limestone plain, there is an infinite variety of fishing available to the Irish angler. This fishing is part of our heritage.

Much of the fishing is either free, or controlled by angling associations whose ranks are open to all, at subscriptions that are often nominal, and never more than the angler of even the most moderate means can afford; and which exist solely for the purpose of conserving and improving the fishing in the interest of sport in their own time, and for the generations of anglers who will follow them. This reflects an attitude towards fishing which is also part of our heritage.

A growing realisation of the importance of angling as a national amenity has resulted in the setting up, two years ago, of a body whose constitution and policy alike represent an unique experiment in fishery conservation. This body, the Inland Fisheries Trust, was set up by the Government for the development of angling, and in particular brown trout angling, in Ireland. Governed by a Council composed of official representatives nominated because of their technical knowledge or administrative experienc of fishery problems, and of elected representatives, it is an organisation which is open to all. Established, not to supplant angling associations, but to supplement and co-ordinate their efforts to improve angling, it is empowered to acquire waters by gift, purchase or lease, or by other voluntary arrangement, and to hold them in trust for the nation; to carry out research into fishery problems; and to engage in protection and development work beyond the scope of any one voluntary organisation, working on its own.

The limestone lakes—Conn and Arrow, Corrib and Mask. Derg and Ree, Sheelin and Derravaragh, Owel and Ennel—are amongst the most important angling waters in the country. In 1952, on Lough Sheelin, one of the waters acquired by the Trust, investigations were begun into the biological and practical problems involved in the improvement of brown trout fishing in waters of this type. A certain amount of data from some of the other lakes was obtained and considered. There were on-the-spot discussions with angling associations and experienced local anglers. Finally, in November, 1952, trout from Lough Feagh, near Newport, Co. Mayo, were made available, through the generosity of the owner of the fishery, to the

## WORLD TROUT FLY FISHING COMPETITION. 21

Castlebar Anglers' Association, and were transferred to Lough Conn in a joint operation in which the Association, the Fisheries Branch of the Department of Agriculture (who tagged the fish in connection with an investigation into the growth of trout in acid and alkaline waters), and the Trust took part.

The outcome has been the formation of a scheme, administered by the Trust and financed by An Bord Failte, for the improvement of brown trout fishing in Corrib, Mask, Conn and Arrow. It is being worked with the co-operation of the local angling associations and provides for the reduction of predatory coarse fish stocks by netting, trapping and electrical fishing, and for the transplantation of trout from over-stocked waters elsewhere to the rich feeding of the limestone lakes.

In these vast sheets of water, miracles will not be worked overnight. There are many problems which will need to be solved, and many difficulties will arise. But, if enthusiasm and initiative count for anything, the ultimate success of the scheme can scarcely be doubted. For enthusiasm and initiative are qualities in which the angling associations, which will play a major part in the scheme, are certainly not lacking. This will be evident to readers of these pages; and both as Secretary of the Trust, and as a fellow-angler, I would like to take this opportunity of wishing the Castlebar Anglers every success in the enterprise which forms the subject of this brochure, and which is typical of this energetic and imaginative Association.

MICHAEL KENNEDY.

*Exit from Cushlough to Lough Mask.*

# BALLINROBE.

BALLINROBE, situated on the southern shore of Lough Mask, is an ideal centre for the angler. There is, between guest house and hotel, first-class accommodation for guests, while ghillies and boats are readily available on request. Apart from the excellent fishing on Lough Mask, the River Robe, running through the town, is recognised as one of the foremost fisheries in the country, particularly that stretch of it from the town to Hollymount, where trout f 5, 6, 7 and 8 lbs. have been taken.

There is an active Angling Association in the town, the members of which will gladly do all they can to facilitate visitors and ensure that their stay is a pleasant one. Apart from anglers and angling, the people of Ballinrobe are noted for their hospitality, and a really traditional Irish welcome awaits the visitor, male or female, young or old, who comes here during 1953.

Ballinrobe extends to all a cead mile failte, with the hope that, whatever centre you choose for the big competition, you'll at least pay this old town a visit.

## LOUGH MASK AND ITS TROUT.

I CAST my memory back to that glorious summer of 1921. Nine weeks of blazing sunshine with hardly a shower of rain. Lough Mask was a shimmering lake of silver, with the Tourmakeady mountains reflected in its waters—a peaceful scene.

I caught my first Masker that season on the wet fly: a short, thick speckled beauty of 1½ lbs. If my memory serves me right, it was on the Invicta.

I remember quite distinctly the exact spot I hooked the trout: it was within a yard or two of the rocky shore of Colmcille's Island. On this island are some ancient ruins. In after years I made it my camping ground.

My boatman and friend for some years was that prince of boatmen, the late Pat Horan, of Derrymore, Partry. I was destined to have many, many pleasant days on the lake with Pat, and many good catches of trout and pike, with his knowledge and skill in handling his boat to help me.

Pat was a boatman in a thousand. On bad days, with nothing doing, he was always ready with an angling yarn to while away the time. His favourite true story, and one of the first he related to me, is remarkable in itself. Pat was out with two Westport anglers one day during the May fly season of 1915. The lake was almost flat calm. As his boat emerged from the Coone river into the lake proper, he noticed something on the surface about a quarter of a mile away.

Rowing over quietly to the spot, he saw a large pike with a trout crossways in its open jaws and apparently choking the pike. He slipped his net neatly under the pike and trout and landed both. The trout was alive and bleeding from the gills; it weighed 4 lbs. The pike weighed 20 lbs. They fished all day long and caught not another fish.

Pat always carried in his boat a large circular net of 24 ins. diameter and good hefty gaff. I wish that some of the other boatmen I know would follow his example. Many a fine trout is lost in Lough Mask through the use of small nets, and more especially through the handles being too short. In my opinion anything less than 5 feet is almost useless.

The best time to fish Mask or Carra with wet flies is from the commencement of May to the end of June. Some nice baskets can be caught as early as April. In September, when the trout have gorged on the pike fry and perch fry, they rise fairly freely to the wet fly.

August is the month for dapping the grasshopper and daddy-long-legs. Very few local anglers dap; it is mostly the visiting anglers who indulge in this method of fishing. They are under the impression (erroneously) that it is next to useless to fish Mask with wet flies, consequently they leave all their wet fly tackle at home. Some of the best baskets of trout on Mask are caught on the wet fly.

I will grant that the average weight of trout caught on the dap will be higher than that of the wet fly, but, against that, a greater number of trout will be taken on the wet fly.

There is no comparison from a sporting point of view between dapping and casting. Baskets of 20 trout per rod on wet fly are fairly common on Mask during the May fly season. My best basket was taken after a thunderstorm and consisted of 28 trout from $\frac{1}{2}$lb. to a $4\frac{1}{4}$lbs. gillaroo. All these were caught on a cast of wet flies. I have been sorry on more than one occasion that I did not weight that particular catch. It cannot have been far short of 40 lbs—there were several fish over 2 lbs.

Trout up to 7 lbs. have been caught on the wet fly.

My favourite cast of flies is composed of an artificial winged May fly on the top dropper; middle fly a Golden Olive; tail fly a green hackled green-bodied May fly, which is known locally as a sunk green. In my opinion there is no better cast for Mask, Corrib, Conn or Carra.

A Connemara Black, an Invicta, Green Olive, Claret and Mallard, and an Alexandra for change, are all an angler need worry about in his outfit.

The dressing of my favourite May fly is:—Wing: Yellow upright wings at least $\frac{1}{2}$ an inch high. Body: Yellow silk with black silk rib. Hackle: Ginger (for some unknown reason this hackle kills better than a yellow one). Tail: Three golden pheasant toppings.

The dressing of my favourite Connemara Black is:—Body: Black silk with silver rib. Wing: Dark mallard. Under wing: A strip of red and a strip of blue ibis. Hackle—Black cock and jay mixed. Tip: Claret silk. Tail: Three golden pheasant tippets. The size of the book for May fly is number 8 (old numbers) and for wet flies size 9 (old numbers). A smaller hook is useless.

The dapper has very little to worry about, provided he fits himself out with 20 yards of a good quality silk dapping line spliced to at least 80 yards of backing, a few good quality $1\frac{1}{2}$ yard tapered casts, and, above all, some of the best quality dapping hooks he can buy, either eyed or tied to gut. A wide bend with sharp and quick penetrating barb is the ideal hook. If semi-snecked, so much the better.

The boatmen collect the May flies as required from the back of rocks and bushes. They generally provide a home-made fly box, with its trap-door on top and sides made of perforated zinc.

I would suggest to every angler visiting Lough Mask or any of our big Western lakes to include in his outfit (even if he has to borrow it) a trolling rod—any length over 7 ft. will do. It need not be too stiff in action, but should be hefty enough to deal with a 20 lb. pike. A copper and silver spoon bait or two, not less than 3 inches long, and an Archer spinner big enough to mount a quarter-pound trout on will do for pike.

For trout, I have found nothing better than a 2-inch Gold Devon as an all-round killer.

One of the reasons I have suggested that visiting anglers should include trolling tackle in their outfits when visiting Lough Mask for an angling holiday is that on the off-day, when there is nothing doing on the wet fly or the dap, and the lake is almost rippleless, the trolling outfit may make all the difference between an empty creel and a peace offering in the form of a good pike or, more esteemed still in most households, a Mask trout of no mean proportions. Yes, you start in the hall-door with a feeling of confidence. After visiting the various halls on the way home, as we say in the West of Ireland, "you can't pass the neighbours' children," especially if liquid refreshments are up to the mark. Many a big trout lives to-day which was killed on the way home.

It is only within the past 15 yeas that pike and perch fishing has been taken seriously as a form of sport in this country. We know next to nothing about coarse fishing. Across the water coarse fishing forms the chief sport for the majority of anglers. Pike, perch, bream, roach, etc., claim thousands of anglers who have become adepts at float-fishing, live-baiting, spinning, etc. What an anglers' paradise awaits them here in the West of Ireland. Pike of over 40 lbs. have been caught on Lough Mask; perch up to 4 lbs.

The biggest pike I had in my possession was a female fish of 36 lbs., beautifully proportioned, caught on a 4-inch Blue and Silver Wagtail in the Cloone river at Derrymore, just as the river enters Lough Mask. My record day's pike fishing was 13 pike with a 4¼ lb. trout thrown in for luck. My companion had 4 pike, making in all 17 pike and a 4¼ trout. I believe that this is a record for one boat.

The biggest authentic trout caught on Mask was one of 18¾ lbs. by Mr. Pat O'Malley, Clonbur, taken on a large copper and silver spoon. A trout of 14 lbs.—a fine, handsome specimen hen fish, only 8¼ years old—was caught on the 7th May, 1950, off Devenish Island, by Mr. William W. Hewetson (Westport) on a small Golden Plastic Devon, gut trace and two-piece spinning rod. This was the largest trout taken for over 20 years.

The largest trout killed on the dap was almost 14 lbs. weight. A handsome specimen of 10 lbs. 2 oz. was caught by Dr. Gibson

Thornton in May, 1945, near Croely bay, and played for over an hour.

At this stage it may not be amiss to give some of the results of the Mask Championship contests:

**LOUGH MASK CHAMPIONSHIPS (WET FLY ONLY).**

June 10, 1935. 48 Rods. 138 Tout.

| Prize. | Trout. | lbs. | ozs. | Best Trout lbs. | ozs. |
|---|---|---|---|---|---|
| 1st | 13 | 7 | 6 | | |
| 2nd | 8 | 5 | 14 | 1 | 15¾ |
| 3rd | 6 | 5 | 13 | 1 | 7¼ |
| 4th | 4 | 4 | 15½ | 1 | 14 |

May 24, 1936. 20 Rods. 73 Trout.

| Prize. | Trout. | lbs. | ozs. | Best Trout lbs. | ozs. |
|---|---|---|---|---|---|
| 1st | 7 | 9 | 2 | 2 | 14 |
| 2nd | 4 | 8 | ½ | 3 | 9 |
| 3rd | 5 | 5 | 6 | | |
| 4th | 3 | 4 | 12 | 3 | 4½ |
| | 19 | 27 | 11½ | 3—9 | 12 |

A fine average.

In my opinion this is a record for averages on any lake in Ireland in competitions.

May 30, 1937. 20 Rods. 57 Trout.

| Prize. | Trout. | lbs. | ozs. | Best Trout lbs. | ozs. |
|---|---|---|---|---|---|
| 1st | 7 | 9 | 2¾ | 2 | 11¼ |
| 2nd | 11 | 7 | 10½ | | |
| 3rd | 8 | 6 | 11 | 2 | 4¼ |
| 4th | 2 | 5 | 0½ | 3 | 4¼ |
| 5th | 5 | 4 | 10 | 2 | 9½ |

May 29, 1938. 42 Rods. 102 Trout.

| Prize. | Trout. | lbs. | ozs. | Best Trout lbs. | ozs. |
|---|---|---|---|---|---|
| 1st | 13 | 9 | 9½ | | |
| 2nd | 12 | 8 | | | |
| 3rd | 3 | 5 | 8¾ | 2 | 12¾ |
| 4th | 6 | 5 | 12 | | |
| 5th | 7 | 4 | 8½ | | |

I will now skip a few years to give the results of the last two competitions held, in order to shorten this article and to show that Mask has not fallen back in results.

The National fell by the way in choosing unsuitable dates. The Mask Championship is run by the Westport and District Anglers' Club with a local Hon. Secretary.

## 32 WORLD TROUT FLY FISHING COMPETITION.

Mr. W. W. Hewetson, with 28 trout from ½ lb. to 4½ lb. Gillaroo, which he took with wet flies in Lively Bay and the shallows south of Seagull Island, on Lough Mask, on May 31, 1931. This catch may be a record for one rod with wet flies in a single day.

| Prize. | May 19, 1940. Trout. | 22 Rods. lbs. | 64 Trout. ozs. | Best Trout lbs. ozs. | |
|---|---|---|---|---|---|
| 1st | 6 | 6 | 9½ | 1 | 10½ |
| 2nd | 8 | 5 | 11¾ | | |
| 3rd | 6 | 5 | 0¼ | | |
| 4th | 8 | 4 | 15¾ | | |
| 5th | 2 | 3 | 5¼ | 2 | 1¾ |

| Prize. | June 6, 1943. Trout. | 20 Rods. lbs. | 59 Trout. ozs. | Best Trout lbs. ozs. | |
|---|---|---|---|---|---|
| 1st | 13 | 9 | 6½ | 2 | 2 |
| 2nd | 9 | 6 | 0 | | |
| 3rd | 6 | 5 | 12¾ | 3 | 11½ |
| 4th | 9 | 5 | 12½ | | |
| 5th | 5 | 4 | 5½ | 1 | 15½ |

# WORLD TROUT FLY FISHING COMPETITION.

The results given of the Lough Mask Championships have not been excelled or equalled by any other angling contests held in Eire.

The best centres to fish Lough Mask from are: Cahir Pier, Clonbur, Partry, Kilbride, Tourmakeady and Aughnigh.

Boatmen now understand that they must provide their own lunch; it is optional whether that is augmented by the angler. In the good old days we used to bring half a dozen "largers" for the boatman and forget the corkscrew as often as not. The charge for boat and man is £1 per day.

Boats are 18 ft. long and specially built for Lough Mask, easy to handle and absolutely safe in a gale of wind. The boatmen are expert and know every inch of the water. Anglers may place implicit faith in their boatman—he will do his utmost to get you fish by hook crook or net. They are a fine bunch of fellows.

A movement is now on foot for stocking Mask, Corrib, Conn and Carra with small trout up to half-pound from the numerous small lakes in Connemara which abound in small underfed trout. Numbers of these lakes have never been fished and are in themselvs natural rearing ponds.

CONNEMARA BLACK.

# WORLD TROUT FLY FISHING COMPETITION.
## LOUGH CORRIB.

I HAVE been asked by the organisers of the International Trout Fly Fishing Competition, during An Tostal, to write a few words about fly fishing on Lough Corrib.

I approach the subject with much trepidation, knowing well that I shall be chewed into small pieces by the many experienced anglers who abound the shores of the Corrib both in and around Oughterard, as well as those of our small community of "foreigners" who, with or without experience, know all there is, and a bit more, about the habits of, and lures for, the wary brown trout.

Angling on the Corrib or any other lough can always be a chancy business, and, according to hearsay, especially in the bar at night, there are always plenty of fish in some bay, or off some island, where you were yesterday (and never had even a touch), and if you query the accuracy of such a statement you are immediately shown as fine a basket of sizeable trout as you have seen for some time. Of course, there is always the 7- or 8-pounder which got away. But it does not do to be too sceptical, because one learns that the seemingly impossible happens frequently.

In my humble opinion, anglers can be divided into two categories : first, the angler whose very life and existence would appear to depend on the weight and number of his kill, and, if he has a bad day, he either goes to bed and will talk with no one, or will come into the bar and tell all and sundry that they are wasting time on the Corrib; and the second type, who goes out cheerfully in any conditions and probably fishes hard with little or no luck, but who comes in in the evening brimming over with "joie de vivre," calls for a jar and is loud in his praise of an open air life and the fact that there is always a to-morrow. This latter type gets all there is to be got out of fishing (with its camaradie), and is frequently by far the better angler. Would that there were more of them!

One could go on for hours dividing and sub-dividing these types, for, after spending only one season on the wrong side of the bar in an angling community, one learns an awful lot about one's fellow-men. It will be noticed that I have not said a word about the ladies, God bless 'em! Why? Just because I would not dare, and I have no wish to become "corpus delicti" even at my ripe old age.

MAXWELL ROBERTS, Colonel.

*7th World Trout Competition, Lough Mask, Co. Mayo. Competitors all set for the push-off.*

*All celebrate a worthy Champion, 1953.*

*Bob Church, Northampton; Brendan Smith, Sligo, 1983 Champion; Dermot Treacy, Sligo, 1971 Winner and representing E.S.B. Sponsorship with John Nestor, Chairman.*

*Martin Calvey looks on anxiously before the "Off".*

*From left: John Joyce, Manager Bank of Ireland, Ballinrobe, with Committee members Dominic Curran, Ray Owens, Anthony McCormack and Noel Finlay, at launch of Millennium Competition.*

*Discussing tactics before the "Off".*

*Late evening fishing Maam Trasna, Lough Mask.*

*Padraig Munroe, 1997 Winner thinks he has the "killer fly" – Martin Feerick has other ideas.*